SMP interact 9T

Teacher's guide to Book 9T

Contents

CAMBRIDGE UNIVERSITY PRESS

CAMBRIDGE UNIVERSITY PRESS
Cambridge, New York, Melbourne, Madrid, Cape Town, Singapore, São Paulo

Cambridge University Press
The Edinburgh Building, Cambridge CB2 8RU, UK

www.cambridge.org
Information on this title: www.cambridge.org/9780521538206

© The School Mathematics Project 2003

First published 2003
4th printing 2007

Printed in the United Kingdom at the University Press, Cambridge

A catalogue record for this publication is available from the British Library

ISBN 978-0-521-53820-6 paperback

Typesetting and technical illustrations by The School Mathematics Project
Cover image © ImageState Ltd
Cover design by Angela Ashton

The following people contributed to the writing of the SMP Interact key stage 3 materials.

Ben Alldred	Ian Edney	John Ling	Susan Shilton
Juliette Baldwin	Steve Feller	Carole Martin	Caroline Starkey
Simon Baxter	Rose Flower	Peter Moody	Liz Stewart
Gill Beeney	John Gardiner	Lorna Mulhern	Pam Turner
Roger Beeney	Bob Hartman	Mary Pardoe	Biff Vernon
Roger Bentote	Spencer Instone	Peter Ransom	Jo Waddingham
Sue Briggs	Liz Jackson	Paul Scruton	Nigel Webb
David Cassell	Pamela Leon	Richard Sharpe	Heather West

Others, too numerous to mention individually, gave valuable advice, particularly by commenting on and trialling draft materials.

Editorial team	**Project administrator**	**Design**	**Project support**
David Cassell	Ann White	Pamela Alford	Carol Cole
Spencer Instone		Melanie Bull	Pam Keetch
John Ling		Nicky Lake	Jane Seaton
Paul Scruton		Tiffany Passmore	Cathy Syred
Susan Shilton		Martin Smith	
Caroline Starkey			
Heather West			

Special thanks go to Colin Goldsmith.

Introduction

Teaching approaches

SMP Interact sets out to help teachers use a variety of teaching approaches in order to stimulate pupils and foster their understanding and enjoyment of mathematics.

A central place is given to discussion and other interactive work. In this respect and others the material supports the methodology of the *Framework for teaching mathematics*. Questions that promote effective discussion and activities well suited to group work occur throughout the material.

Some activities, mostly where a new idea or technique is introduced, are described only in the teacher's guide. (These are indicated in the pupils' book by a solid marginal strip – see below.)

Materials

There are three series in key stage 3: books 7T–9T cover up to national curriculum level 5; 7S–9S go up to level 6; 7C–9C go up to level 7, though schools have successfully prepared pupils for level 8 with them, drawing lightly on extra topics from early in the *SMP Interact* GCSE course.

Pupils' books

Each unit of work begins with a statement of learning objectives and most units end with questions for self-assessment.

Teacher-led activities that are described in the teacher's guide are denoted by a solid marginal strip in both the pupil's book and the teacher's guide.

Some other activities that are expected to need teacher support are marked by a broken strip.

Where the writers have particular classroom organisation in mind (for example working in pairs or groups), this is stated in the pupils' book.

Resource sheets

Resource sheets, some essential and some optional, are linked to some activities in the books.

Practice booklets

For each book there is a practice booklet containing further questions unit by unit. These booklets are particularly suitable for homework.

Teacher's guides

For each unit, there is usually an overview, details of any essential or optional equipment, including resource sheets, and the practice booklet page references, followed by guidance that includes detailed descriptions of teacher-led activities, advice on difficult ideas and comments from teachers who trialled the material.

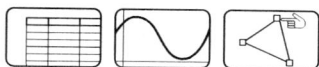

There is scope to use computers and graphic calculators throughout the material. These symbols mark specific opportunities to use a spreadsheet, graph plotter and dynamic geometry software respectively.

Answers to questions in the pupils' book and the practice booklet follow the guidance. For reasons of economy answers to resource sheets that pupils write on are not always given in the teacher's guide; they can of course be written on a spare copy of the sheet.

Assessment

Unit by unit assessment tests are available both as hard copy and as editable files on CD (details are at www.smpmaths.org.uk). The practice booklets are also suitable as an assessment resource.

Oral and mental starters

An oral and mental starter can be used for a number of purposes.

- It can **introduce the main topic**.
- It can also be an effective way of **revising skills that are needed for the main topic**.
- Alternatively it can be used **to 'keep alive' skills learned earlier that are unrelated to the main lesson**.

The 'Number bites' (pages 4–9 of the pupils' book) can be adapted into revision starters.

Many of the teacher-led activities described in this guide can be used as starters, for example unit 8 'Garden centre' (p 47 of the pupils' book) and unit 14 'Bottles' (p 83), which can both be used more than once, and unit 2 'Clock polygons' (p 10), for which extra questions can easily be made up.

Starters can also be based on questions in the pupils' book, specially those where items are displayed, for example B1 on p 12, where you could add more questions or display different vegetable prices on the board.

Starter formats

The formats that follow have been found very effective and can be adapted to different topics.

Show me

Ask, say, 'Show me a factor of 6'. Pupils write their answer on a small whiteboard, or choose a card from a prepared set and show it to you, giving you instant feedback on the whole class. 'Show me boards' work well with other types of starter, such as *True or false?*, and *Odd one out*.

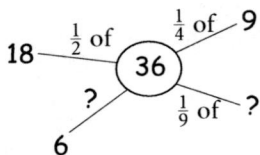

Today's number is …
Write a number on the board and put a ring round it. Pupils make up calculations that have that number as their result.

$\frac{1}{2}$ of → 18 $\frac{1}{4}$ of → 9

(36)

? → 6 $\frac{1}{9}$ of → ?

Spider diagram
Write a number, word or expression in a circle on the board (the 'body'). The 'legs' can show operations, and pupils put the results at the 'feet'.

Array
Show a grid or list of numbers. Pupils have to perform operations on them or choose answers to questions you pose from them.

Display
Display a diagram, graph, calculation, etc. (an OHP transparency is often ideal); ask questions about it or ask pupils to make statements about it.

Odd one out
Display a set of numbers, times, words, or shapes etc. Pupils have to identify the odd one out.

Counting stick
The stick is marked in alternately coloured graduations and can be used for a range of counting-on and number line activities.

True or false?
Pupils have to decide if statements are true or false (see the examples on page 123 of the pupils' book).

Loop cards
Each card has a question on it and the answer to a question on another card; the complete set forms a loop. One pupil reads out their question; the pupil with the answer responds and reads out their question, and so on.

Bingo
You 'call' questions and pupils cross off answers that are on their individual 'bingo' card.

Around the world
One pupil stands behind another. You ask them a question. Whoever answers first then stands behind a different pupil, and so on.

Matching
Pupils have to match items that are the same. Each pupil could be given a card with an item on and then find who has the card that matches theirs.

Target number
For example, give the class four random digits. Pupils have to write a calculation which is as close as possible to a given target.

Ordering
Pupils put items in order, for example, a set of rectangles in order of area. The items could be on large cards, held up by a group of pupils at the front, who have to arrange themselves in the right order.

Hot seat
Three pupils sit at the front in the hot seats. The rest of the class formulate questions on a particular topic to ask the panel.

Topics for starters

These are related to work in 9T. The corresponding sections in the teacher's guides to 7T and 8T will be useful to review earlier work.

Multiplication and division

Spider diagram Pupils multiply or divide the body number by numbers on the legs.

Array Pupils multiply or divide each number on a grid by 10, 100 or 1000.

Fractions and percentages

Spider diagram Put a number, for example 48, in the body and have '$\frac{1}{4}$ of', '$\frac{1}{3}$ of' etc. on the legs; or put a percentage in the body and values on the legs and feet as shown here.

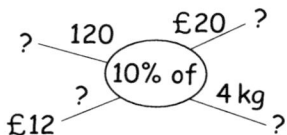

Matching/Odd one out Ask pupils to match pairs of equivalent fractions in a list or spot the non-equivalent one.

Today's number is … Give 1 as the number, or give a fraction less than 1.

Number relationships

Show me Give out a set of cards with, say, 1 to 30 on them, one to each pupil. Ask for a factor of 48, a prime number, a square number, the square root of 36 etc.; pupils show their card if it fits the description.

Bingo Multiples and factors bingo is described in section B of unit 17 'Number relationships'.

Matching Make a set of cards that include all the factors of, say, 60 and some numbers that are not factors; pupils get one card each. Ask them to put themselves in pairs that multiply to give 60; those that can't sit down and hold their number up.

Time

Display Use a simple timetable as the basis for questions.

Spider diagram Put a time in the middle and on the legs have '10 minutes after' and so on.

Matching Show pupils a list of times in different formats and ask them to match pairs of times that are the same.

Ratio

Spider diagram Use an approach like this.

Display On an OHP place 'coloured counters' that have been drawn on a transparency and cut out. Pupils have to give the ratio of one colour to another.

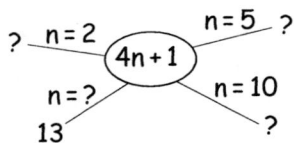

Algebra

Spider diagram Place an expression in the body and values of the variable on the legs.

Matching Ask pupils to match pairs of equivalent expressions such as $n + n + n + 3 + 5$ and $3n + 5$. Alternatively ask them to match expressions to the perimeter and area of shapes like those in question A2 of unit 18 'Simplifying' (p 100).

Odd one out Give pupils a list of expressions with an odd one out. This can reveal common misconceptions such as $3n = 3 + n$.

Angle

Display Display angles on an OHP; pupils estimate their size.

Matching Pupils match pairs of complementary angles, supplementary angles, and angles that fit around a point. Alternatively prepare some cards, each showing a single angle, but with the whole set consisting of groups of three that are angles of a triangle; each pupil gets one card and has to find the other two angles that make up a triangle: a challenge!

Array Show some angles between 0° and 180°. Ask questions such as 'Which of the angles is complementary to 54°?' and 'Which would be the third angle in a triangle if the other two were 50° and 65°?'

Coordinates

Bingo Each pupil draws a grid labelled ⁻3 to 3 on each axis. They choose and mark seven points with little circles; this is their bingo card. You have a grid too and call out coordinates of points at random.

Display Show a coordinate grid labelled ⁻3 to 3 on each axis, for use as a 'four in line' board. The class is in two teams, each with a team colour. The teams take turns to give the coordinates of a point, which is then marked with their colour. The first team with four points in a line wins.

Area and perimeter

Matching Show pupils a set of rectangles with given dimensions. Ask them to match pairs that have the same area or perimeter.

Ordering Pupils put a set of rectangles or composite shapes in order of increasing area or perimeter.

Transformations

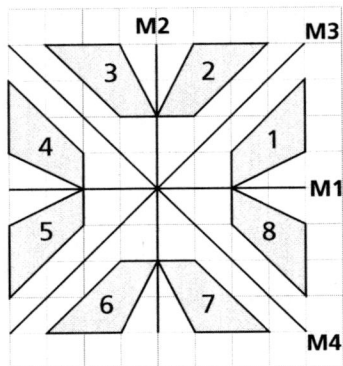

Display Use a diagram of the kind shown here. Ask pupils which shape is the reflection of shape 2 in the line M1, etc.

Probability

Display Show pictures of spinners or marbles under cups. Ask questions such as 'Which spinner has a probability of $\frac{4}{7}$ of red winning?' Alternatively write probabilities as well and use the *Matching* format.

Pie charts

Display Show pie charts of the types used in unit 11 and ask about the information they give.

① Number bites

This consists of 18 activities based on number skills covered in earlier SMP Interact materials. **These are intended as a resource to be dipped into throughout this book and are not meant to be worked through as a single unit.**

A wide range of activities are included: written questions, oral work, puzzles and investigations. Many of the activities can be used in a variety of ways, as class activities, group work or individual tasks. It is hoped that the wide range of activities may suggest to teachers similar activities they could design themselves.

All the activities are expected to be done without the use of a calculator.

The activities are mainly grouped into whole numbers, fractions and decimals, and the order of the activities roughly represents an order of progression. Some units later in this book rely on some of the skills practised here and these may therefore provide useful revision practice for weaker pupils immediately prior to starting these later units.

> **Essential**
>
> Sheets 266, 267, scissors

W Whole numbers (p 4)

> Sheet 266, scissors (for W6)

F Fractions (p 6)

D Decimals (p 7)

> Sheet 267

D3 Telephone pole

The purpose of this activity is to provide practice in adding and multiplying decimals with one decimal place. By comparing their total distances with others in the class pupils should be encouraged to seek an optimum solution. The optimum position gives a total scale length of about 30.5 cm, or 152.5 m on the ground.

Ⓜ **A mixed bag** (p 9)

M2 Day and night

The data given can be used to ask questions orally on the differences between the temperatures in the rooms during the day and at night. Begin with questions which involve only positive numbers and progress to those which involve negative numbers. Ask questions of the type:

• How much warmer was it in the kitchen than the garden at noon?

• By how much did the temperature drop in the garage between noon and midnight?

• By 6 a.m. the temperature in the garden had dropped 2 degrees below what it was at midnight. What was the temperature at 6 a.m.?

Ⓦ **Whole numbers** (p 4)

W1 Two-digit numbers

1 Here are two solutions:

multiple of 3 is 36, multiple of 5 is 25, multiple of 7 is 14;

multiple of 3 is 36, multiple of 5 is 15, multiple of 7 is 42.

There are six other possibilities.

2 The only solutions are:

multiple of 7 is 35, multiple of 8 is 64, multiple of 9 is 72;

multiple of 7 is 35, multiple of 8 is 64, multiple of 9 is 27;

multiple of 7 is 63, multiple of 8 is 72, multiple of 9 is 45;

multiple of 7 is 63, multiple of 8 is 72, multiple of 9 is 54.

3 There are many sets of three 2-digit numbers which are multiples of 8; for example:

96, 80, 72   80, 72, 16   80, 56, 32

It is impossible to find a set of four 2-digit numbers.

W2 Chairs

No, 450 chairs are needed.

(a) Yes (384)   (b) No (432)

(c) Yes (420)   (d) No (441)

(e) Yes (420)   (f) Yes (418)

W3 Leave it out!

The pupil's calculations
Some examples are:

$$270 \div 2 = 135$$

(a) $136 + 111 = 247$

(b) $5 \times 39 + 6 = 201$

(c) $(8 + 5) \times (8 + 5) = 169$

(d) $3 \times (3 + 1) \times 35 = 420$

(e) $29 \times 12 = 348$

W4 Clues

1 444

2 11

3 177

4 235

5 165

W5 Sporty words

1 POT (712)

2 GOLD (4105)

3 TRAP (2937)

4 GOLF (4108)

5 ROLL (9100)

6 POLO (7101)

7 START (62 392)

8 DARTS (53 926)

W6 Cover up

This is one solution; there are others.

multiples of 3	multiples of 4	odd numbers	
factors of 24		square numbers	factors of 20
prime numbers		even numbers	

𝔽 Fractions (p 6)

F1 What fraction?

(a) $\frac{1}{4}$ (b) $\frac{5}{6}$ (c) $\frac{3}{4}$

(d) $\frac{4}{9}$ (e) $\frac{3}{10}$ (f) $\frac{6}{16} = \frac{3}{8}$

F2 Fractions of words

1 PRIME

2 KITE

3 FACTOR

4 FRACTION

5 POLYGON

F3 A fraction of time

1 (a) 15 min   (b) 30 min

  (c) 6 min   (d) 10 min

  (e) 45 min   (f) 42 min

  (g) 40 min   (h) 25 min

2 (a) $\frac{1}{3}$ (b) $\frac{1}{5}$ (c) $\frac{1}{12}$ (d) $\frac{7}{12}$

𝔻 Decimals (p 7)

D1 Number patterns

1 3.4 4 4.6

2 3.2 3.5 3.8

3 (a) 2.1 2.3   (b) 3.3 3.6

  (c) 9.9 10.3   (d) 6.8 7

  (e) 7.9 7.7   (f) 5.4 5

D2 Bottles

1 (a) 2 litres   (b) 10.5 litres

  (c) 14.4 litres

2 (a) 37.6 litres   (b) 51.2 litres

  (c) 16.2 litres   (d) 5.4 litres

D3 Telephone pole

(a) 12.9 cm   (b) 64.5 m

(c) PB = 9.9 cm (49.5 m)
    PC = 9.4 cm (47 m)

(d) 161 m approx

(e) The pupil's attempt

(f) The optimum position gives a total length of about 30.5 cm (152.5 m).

D4 Missing digits

1
```
   2.8
 + 4.3
   7.1
```

2
```
   1.6
 + 1.5
   3.1
```

3
```
   4.3
 + 3.8
   8.1
```

4
```
   9.3
 - 2.7
   6.6
```

5	8.4 − 1.**3** **7**.1	6	**3**.7 − 2.**4** 1.3
7	7.3 − 2.**8** **4**.5	8	7.**4** − 4.**5** 2.9
9	9.**1** − **0**.5 8.6	10	**8.0** − 2.4 5.6

D5 What's missing?

1 $10 \times 6.3 = \mathbf{63}$

2 $3.1 \times \mathbf{100} = 310$

3 $420 \div 10 = 42$

4 $0.89 \times 10 = 8.9$

5 $6.07 \times \mathbf{100} = 607$

6 $0.03 \times \mathbf{100} = 3$

7 $4 \div \mathbf{100} = 0.04$

8 $0.86 \times \mathbf{100} = 86$

9 $\mathbf{40.2} \div 100 = 0.402$

D6 Made to measure

1 (a) 1.74 m   (b) 1.89 m   (c) 1.96 m
   (d) 2.03 m   (e) 2.17 m   (f) 2.35 m

2 (a) Gill (1.09 m)   (b) Gill (35.82 kg)
       Dean (1.42 m)   Dean (50.7 kg)
       Hitesh (1.57 m)   Farnaz (59 kg)
       Farnaz (1.6 m)   Becky (65.2 kg)
       Becky (1.66 m)   Hitesh (65.26 kg)
       Alan (1.74 m)   Alan (74.65 kg)
       Carl (1.8 m)   Erik (80.71 kg)
       Erik (2.02 m)   Carl (84.12 kg)

D7 Halfway numbers

1 0.2

2 0.3

3 0.25

4 0.15

5 0.95

6 0.5

7 3.5

8 1.3

9 1.2

10 1.25

11 3.15

12 3.05

13 12.5

14 9.05

15 0.35

16 12.05

Ⓜ A mixed bag (p 9)

M1 Last orders

1 14, 17, 20, 23, **26**, 29, **32**, 35

2 18, 25, 32, **39**, **46**, 53, 60

3 0.1, 0.4, 0.7, **1.0**, 1.3, **1.6**, 1.9

4 ⁻10, **⁻7**, ⁻4, **⁻1**, 2, 5, 8

② Clock polygons (p 10)

The work in this unit can be used to help pupils develop mathematical imagery. It also provides an opportunity to revise the names of special types of triangles and quadrilaterals. The concept of congruence is introduced.

Essential	Optional
Sheet 268	Tracing paper
Angle measurer	Transparency of one ring from sheet 268

◊ This material can be used to develop pupils' ability in mathematical imagery. Ask the pupils to close their eyes and imagine a clockface and where the hour numbers will lie. Once the idea of the points around the clockface has been introduced, pupils can be asked to imagine shapes by giving them points such as 9, 6, 12 to be joined up. Once they have all done this, ask questions such as:

• How many sides has it got?

• What lines of symmetry does it have?

• Which side/angle is the biggest?

A detailed description and further activities using this approach are given in SMP 11–16 *Developing mathematical imagery* (CUP 1994).

◊ After doing some examples in their heads as above, pupils can be given a copy of sheet 268. A transparency based on sheet 268 can be used as a basis for class discussion.

Some pupils may take a while to realise that the order the numbers are given in does not matter. Once this is established encourage pupils to quote the points in numerical order. This is useful in discussing congruence. To establish congruence pupils could trace the triangles and check against those they think are the same.

◊ This material could be used to investigate the number sequences that form particular types of triangle. For example, to make a right-angled triangle two of the points must be on opposite ends of a diameter (6 apart). Some 'clock' arithmetic may need to be used: for example the difference between 11 and 2 is 3.

◊ Investigating quadrilaterals may be hard for some pupils and may be omitted.

③ Decimals

Pupils revise multiplication of amounts of money by whole numbers and decimals. The main emphasis of the unit is division by whole numbers and by decimals. Some non-calculator work is included in sections A and B but after that pupils are expected to use calculators throughout. All answers should be given to the nearest penny.

Number bites D1 to D7 on pages 7 to 9 offer suitable revision for weaker pupils before they start this unit.

p 11	**A** Food for friends	Choosing the correct operation to solve simple problems with money, mainly multiplications or division
p 12	**B** Shopping	Multiplying amounts of money without a calculator
		Multiplying amounts of money by a decimal with a calculator
		Dividing by a whole number to find the unit cost
p 13	**C** Rounding	Review of rounding to the nearest penny
p 14	**D** How much each?	Rounding 'long' decimal amounts of money to the nearest penny
p 16	**E** More for your money	Dividing by a decimal to find the unit cost

---

Essential

Calculators

Practice booklet pages 3 to 7

A **Food for friends** (p 11)

'We discussed different strategies for non-calculator working.'

◊ Ask pupils how much money Gina, Mehmet and Molly will each need for their pizzas. Discuss when to multiply and when to divide and ways for pupils to set out their calculations.

The Pizza House menu can be used as the basis for further questions, which you might wish to give orally. For example:

- Three friends share the cost of a Margherita pizza. How much do they each pay?
- How much will it cost for one Napoletana and two Mushroom pizzas?
- Five friends share the cost of an American pizza. How much do they each pay?

B Shopping (p 12)

◊ The prices could be used as the basis of some oral work:
  - What is the cost of 2 kg of onions?
  - How much would $\frac{1}{2}$ kg of new potatoes cost?

C Rounding (p 13)

Pupils revise rounding amounts of money with three decimal places to the nearest penny.

◊ In your introduction, include examples such as 2.5 kg of wild bird seed (leading to £1.725) to remind them that we round **up** from a halfway point.

◊ Pupils could think about how to give very rough estimates for answers to multiplications. For example: '1 kg of premium bird seed costs £1.10 and 2 kg costs £2.20. So 1.3 kg will cost more than £1.10 but less than £2.20.' This can then be compared with the answer found on a calculator.

D How much each? (p 14)

The teacher-led discussion should establish how to round 'long' decimal amounts of money to the nearest penny.

◊ You could start with some oral work:
  - What is the cost of four single creme eggs?
    How much less do you pay for a pack of four?
  - What would be the total cost of two packs of twelve creme eggs?

◊ Ask pupils to try to find the cost of each egg in the pack of four and the pack of twelve. One way of trying to explain how to round to the nearest penny is to think of the digits after the second decimal place as a 'bit of a penny'. For example, £2.60 ÷ 12 = 0.21666666... On a calculator:

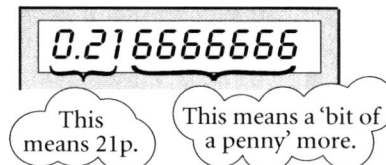

$$0.216666666$$

This means 21p. This means a 'bit of a penny' more.

When the third digit is 5 or above we round up to the nearest penny.
So £0.2166666... = £0.22 or 22p to the nearest penny.

When the third digit is below 5 we round down to the nearest penny.
So £0.97 ÷ 4 = £0.2425 = £0.24 or 24p to the nearest penny.

As an alternative way to cast light upon the process, the calculation can be worked in pence (260p ÷ 12). Then all the figures after the decimal point represent a 'bit of a penny'.

D5 In part (b), pupils have to find the cost per kilogram when given the cost of 0.5 kg. Some may find the cost by doubling and this can be compared with the division method in the next section.

E More for your money (p 16)

◊ You could ask pupils working in groups to find the cost per kilogram for each box of rose food (starting with the largest box) and compare methods. Show pupils that have calculated £0.90 × 2 for the second largest box that £0.90 ÷ 0.5 produces the same result. Some may appreciate that dividing by $\frac{1}{2}$ is equivalent to multiplying by 2, thinking of, say, $8 ÷ \frac{1}{2}$ as 'how many halves in 8?'.

For the third largest box, ask pupils if the cost per kilogram is going to be less than or more than £2.00. Establish that the appropriate calculation is 2 ÷ 1.2 and not 1.2 ÷ 2.

For the smallest box, ask pupils if the cost per kilogram is going to be less than or more than £0.60. Establish that the appropriate calculation is 0.60 ÷ 0.3 and not 0.3 ÷ 0.60.

You may wish to establish the rule:
cost per kilogram = total cost ÷ weight in kilograms.

◊ Introduce the idea of the one 'giving most for your money' being the one with lowest unit cost. Larger items usually work out cheaper per unit cost, but this is not always the case as question E1 illustrates. And of course, if you only need a small amount, then buying a large packet will not necessarily be good value for money.

A Food for friends (p 11)

A1 £24.20

A2 £2.90

A3 £14.40

A4 £1.40

A5 £1.95

A6 £0.85

A7 £1.95

A8 £10.15

B Shopping (p 12)

B1 (a) £4.80   (b) £0.78   (c) £7.00
(d) £5.68   (e) £9.60   (f) £1.56
(g) £8.52   (h) £0.70   (i) £0.26
(j) £4.26

B2 (a) £0.30   (b) £0.31   (c) £0.35

B3 (a) £3.84   (b) £0.91   (c) £7.98
(d) £7.10   (e) £9.36   (f) £1.69
(g) £1.42   (h) £0.42

B4 £0.13

Ⓒ Rounding (p 13)

C1 (a) £1.72   (b) £2.48   (c) £4.54
    (d) £5.28   (e) £2.42   (f) £1.34
    (g) £2.52   (h) £0.72

C2 £0.43

C3 (a) £1.28
    (b) Sunflower seed: £1.51
       Wild bird seed: £0.59
       Premium bird seed: £1.13

Ⓓ How much each? (p 14)

D1 (a) Family: £0.16 or 16p
       Large: £0.12 or 12p
       Giant: £0.11 or 11p
       Jumbo: £0.10 or 10p
    (b) £0.06 or 6p

D2 (a) Free range: £0.21 or 21p
       Standard: £0.13 or 13p
       Economy: £0.07 or 7p
    (b) £0.14 or 14p

D3 A (Light): £0.08 or 8p
     B (Low-fat): £0.20 or 20p

D4 (a) A (Low-fat): £0.27 or 27p
       B (French): £0.25 or 25p
       C (Organic): £0.31 or 31p
       D (Fruit): £0.24 or 24p
    (b) Pack D: Fruit yoghurts

D5 (a) P: £1.99   Q: £1.90   R: £1.75
    (b) X: £1.10   Y: £0.92
    (c) Long grain is cheaper, even in the small bag.

Ⓔ More for your money (p 16)

E1 (a) A: £11.96   B: £9.98
       C: £8.99   D: £9.50
    (b) Pack C (1 kg) gives most.
    (c) The pupil's comments

E2 (a) P: £2.22   Q: £2.00   R: £1.11
    (b) Bag R (25 kg) gives most.

E3 (a) E: £5.00   F: £6.24   G: £9.96
    (b) Pack E (2 kg) gives most.

E4 (a) £1.18   (b) £1.74
    (c) The 5.5 kg bag from Monkfield Ash

E5 (a) X: £2.08   Y: £1.33   Z: £1.18
    (b) 6 kg: £1.40   25 kg: £1.05
    (c) The cheapest way is the 25 kg bag from the gardening catalogue (but of course it isn't cheap if you don't need this amount).

E6 (a) 0.125 litre: £16.80
       0.5 litre: £9.98
       1 litre: £7.99
       5 litres: £4.50
       25 litres: £3.78
    (b) Buy 5 litres and throw away or store the left-over litre.

What progress have you made? (p 18)

1 £5.04

2 £1.64

3 £15.95

4 (a) £5.41   (b) £1.18

5 (a) £0.35   (b) £3.15

6 Family: £0.16 or 16p
   Large: £0.12 or 12p
   Giant: £0.11 or 11p

7 A: £0.39 or 39p
   B: £0.30 or 30p

Practice booklet

Sections A and B (p 3)

1 (a) £5.95   (b) £4.75

2 £2.20

3 (a) £14.25   (b) £7.30   (c) £7.20

4 Baked potato and side salad

5 £9.50 + £10.95 + £3.55 + £7.65
+ £3.60 = £35.25

6 £0.80 or 80p

7 (a) £3.50   (b) £0.14
(c) (i) £5.20   (ii) £4.40
(d) (i) £0.13   (ii) £0.11

Section C (p 4)

1 (a) £10.89   (b) £9.09   (c) £15.08
(d) £3.94   (e) £26.82   (f) £5.03
(g) £3.16   (h) £2.41

2 £6.65

3 (a) £3.95   (b) £10.79
(c) £2.81   (d) £3.48

4 £0.48

5 £2.85

Section D (p 5)

1 (a) (i) £0.24 or 24p
(ii) £0.24 or 24p
(iii) £0.30 or 30p
(iv) £0.26 or 26p
(v) £0.22 or 22p
(vi) £0.31 or 31p
(b) £0.07 or 7p   (c) £0.08 or 8p

2 (a) (i) £0.12 or 12p
(ii) £0.20 or 20p
(iii) £0.24 or 24p
(b) 4p

3 £0.12 or 12p

4 £0.40 or 40p

Section E (p 6)

1 (a) A: £2.30   B: £1.59   C: £1.50
(b) C, the 10 litre can
(c) £11.50   (d) £3.55   (e) £0.95

2 (a) X: £23.80   Y: £16.67   Z: £11.78
(b) Z, the 2.5 litre tin
(c) £17.85   (d) £5.35

3 £11.32

4 (a) £3.96   (b) £4.23
(c) 0.25 litre bottle

Sections C, D and E (p 7)

1 (a) £2.58   (b) £4.13   (c) £2.19
(d) £6.32   (e) £0.90   (f) £1.16

2 (a) £0.27 or 27p   (b) £0.26 or 26p
(c) £0.25 or 25p

3 £0.48 or 48p

4 £0.28 or 28p

5 £0.33 or 33p

6 £1.05

7 (a) Cheddar £6.17
Gouda   £7.23
Stilton   £7.65
(b) Stilton

④ Making rules

Pupils extend patterns or consider situations, and then work out what rule the pattern follows. They express the rule first in words, and later in algebraic shorthand. They also draw graphs from rules.

T	p 19	**A** Rules with words	Forming rules in words from patterns
T	p 22	**B** Rules with letters	Forming rules using letters
T	p 25	**C** Graphs from rules	

Practice booklet pages 8 to 11

Ⓐ **Rules with words** (p 19)

'All the questions were within their capabilities but challenging.'

Use the tea picture to discuss how many spoonfuls of tea would be needed for 4 people, for 6 people, for 1 person, and so on. Record the results systematically in a table.

Ask pupils to give a rule connecting the number of people and the number of spoonfuls. Emphasise that we *know* the number of people; we want to *work out* the number of spoonfuls. So the rule must start

Number of spoonfuls = …

Pupils should be able to spot that the complete rule is

Number of spoonfuls = number of people + 1

You can then discuss finding the rule for the Maori pattern design in a similar way. Look out for pupils who think that because the table 'goes up in twos' therefore the rule must be 'add 2'.

Ⓑ **Rules with letters** (p 22)

'Matches on an OHP helped here.'

◊ The examples in the introduction may be used in a similar way to those at the beginning of section A. Note that example B is the first example in the unit of a set of patterns leading to a rule involving subtraction.

◊ You cannot emphasise too strongly that in rules written like this, the letters stand for *numbers*, and are not shorthand for the objects themselves. So *p* stands for the pattern *number*, and *m* for the *number* of matches.

ℂ **Graphs from rules** (p 25)

◊ Pupils need to make two essential observations from the initial activity:
- When points are plotted from a simple linear rule, as used in this unit, the points will always lie in a straight line.
- The straight line can be used to find other pairs of values which satisfy the rule.

You may wish to point out that only two points are needed in order to draw graphs when the rule gives a straight line. The graph will be more accurate if the two points are at opposite ends of the graph, say $x = 1$ and $x = 10$.

Drawing appropriate scales can be difficult for some pupils so the examples require only simple scales. They should be reminded that scales need labelling and the rule should be written on the graph.

𝔸 **Rules with words** (p 19)

A1 (a) The pupil's patterns 5 and 6

(b)

Pattern number	1	2	3	4	5	6
Number of crosses	3	4	5	6	7	8

(c) 12 crosses   (d) 22

(e) Number of crosses
= pattern number + 2

A2 (a) The pupil's patterns 5 and 6

(b)

Pattern number	1	2	3	4	5	6
Number of crosses	2	4	6	8	10	12

(c) 200 crosses

(d) Number of crosses
= pattern number × 2

A3 Number of crosses = pattern number + 4

A4 A: Number of crosses
= pattern number + 6
There are 106 crosses in pattern 100.

Pattern number	1	2	3	4
Number of crosses	7	8	9	10

B: Number of crosses
= pattern number + 1
There are 101 crosses in pattern 100.

Pattern number	1	2	3	4
Number of crosses	2	3	4	5

C: Number of crosses
= pattern number × 2 + 3
There are 203 crosses in pattern 100.

Pattern number	1	2	3	4
Number of crosses	5	7	9	11

D: Number of crosses
= pattern number × 3 + 1
There are 301 crosses in pattern 100.

Pattern number	1	2	3	4
Number of crosses	4	7	10	13

A5 (a) 3 spoonfuls   (b) 4 spoonfuls

(c) $2\frac{1}{2}$ spoonfuls

(d) Number of spoonfuls
= number of people ÷ 2

A6 (a) 10   (b) 12

(c) 14   (d) 202

(e) Number of motorbikes
= number of cars × 2 + 2

B Rules with letters (p 22)

B1 (a) Pattern 4 uses 8 matches.

(b)

p	1	2	3	4	5	6
m	2	**4**	**6**	**8**	**10**	**12**

(c) Number of matches
= pattern number × 2

(d) $m = 2p$

B2 (a)

p	1	2	3	4	5	6
m	3	4	5	6	7	8

(b) $m = p + 2$

B3 A: $m = 2p + 1$ B: $m = 3p$
C: $m = 4p - 1$

B4 A: $m = 3p + 1$ B: $m = 4p - 3$
C: $m = 5p$ with the pupil's tables

B5 (a) 20 legs, so 5 horses

(b) 3   (c) 25

(d) Divide the number of legs by 4

(e) $h = l \div 4$ or $h = \dfrac{l}{4}$

(The pupils use their own letters.)

B6 (a) $m = 8$

(b, c) The pupil's patterns such as

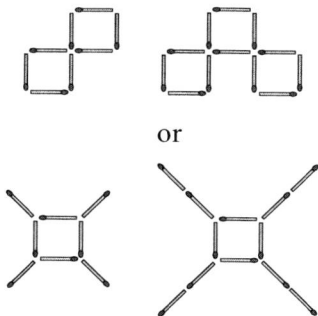

C Graphs from rules (p 25)

C1 (a) 11   (b) 17   (c) 21

C2 (a)

p	1	2	3	4	5
c	5	6	**7**	**8**	**9**

(b) $c = p + 4$

(c) 14

(d), (e)

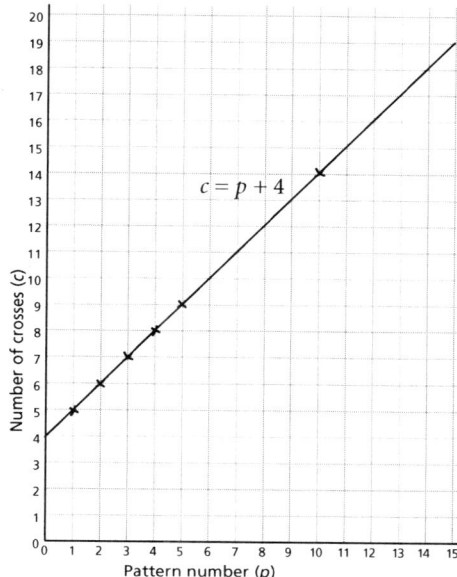

(f) (i) 11   (ii) 17

C3 (a)

p	1	2	3	4	5
n	3	5	**7**	**9**	**11**

(b) 21

(c)

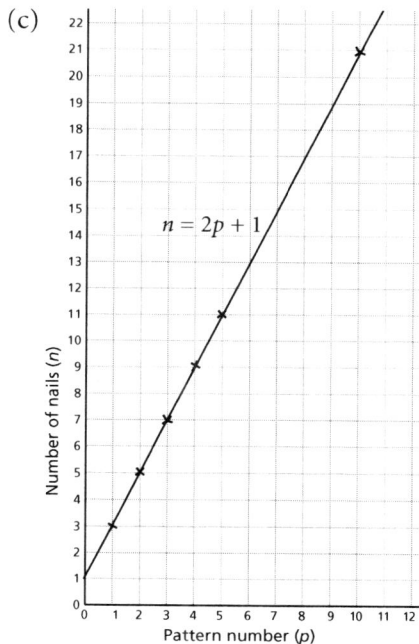

(d) (i) 15   (ii) 23

(e) 9

C4 (a) (i) 4   (ii) 13   (iii) 25

(b)

x	1	2	3	4	5
$y = 3x - 2$	1	4	7	10	13

(c), (d)

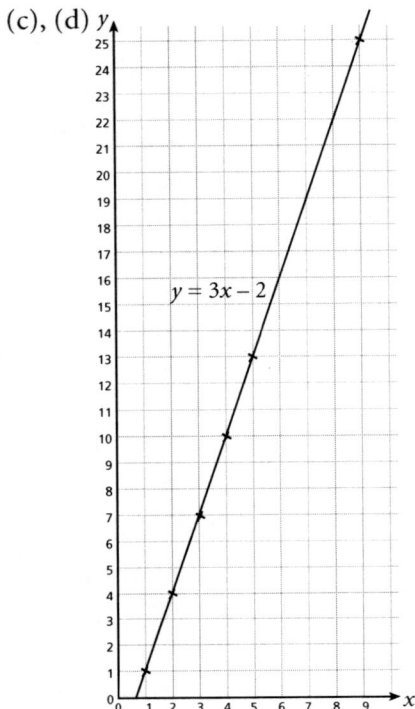

$y = 3x - 2$

(e) 19

The pupil's check that it fits the rule

C5 (a)

Distance (miles)	10	20	30	50	100
Cost in £	50	70	90	130	230

(b)

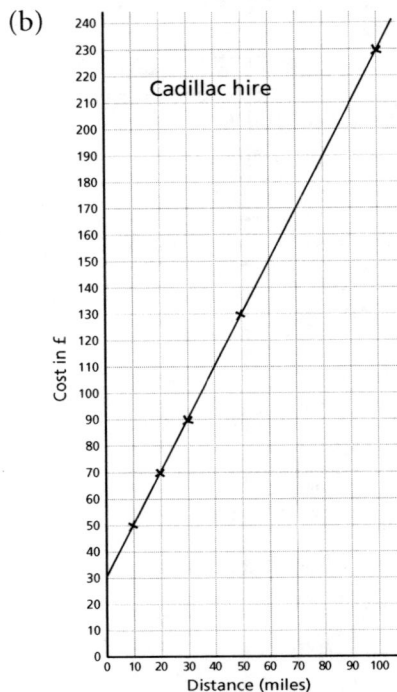

Cadillac hire

(c) £170

(d) 80 miles

What progress have you made? (p 28)

1 (a) Pattern 4   Pattern 5

(b)

Pattern number	1	2	3	4	5
Number of crosses	4	5	6	7	8

(c) 13 crosses

(d) The rule is
Number of crosses = pattern number + 3

2 (a)

p	1	2	3	4	5	6
m	3	6	9	12	15	18

(b) 300 matches   (c) $m = 3p$

3 (a)

x	1	2	3	4	10
$y = 2x + 3$	5	**7**	**9**	**11**	**23**

(b)

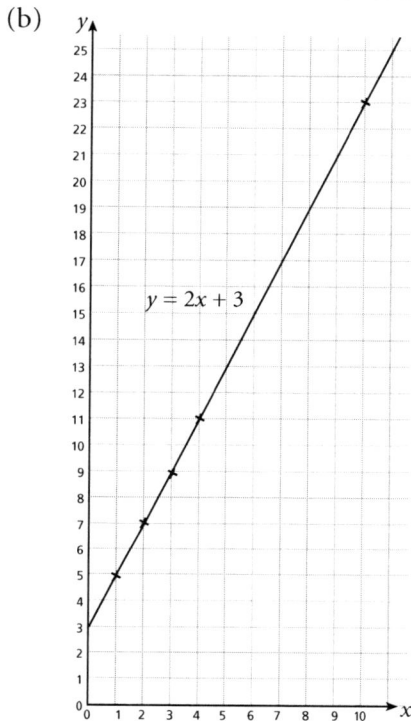

$y = 2x + 3$

2 A:

Pattern number	1	2	3	4
Number of tiles	3	5	7	9

Number of tiles = 2 × pattern number + 1

Pattern 100 has 201 tiles.

B:

Pattern number	1	2	3	4
Number of tiles	3	6	9	12

Number of tiles = 3 × pattern number

Pattern 100 has 300 tiles.

C:

Pattern number	1	2	3	4
Number of tiles	4	7	10	13

Number of tiles = 3 × pattern number + 1

Pattern 100 has 301 tiles.

3 (a) £22

(b) £34

(c) Cost in pounds
= 6 × number of hours + 10

Practice booklet

Section A (p 8)

1 (a)

(b)

Pattern number	1	2	3	4	5
Number of tiles	2	**4**	**6**	**8**	**10**

(c) 20

(d) Number of tiles = pattern number × 2

(e) 200

Section B (p 9)

1 (a) The pupil's pattern 4

(b) 8

(c)

p	1	2	3	4	5
b	2	**4**	**6**	**8**	**10**

(d) $b = 2p$

2 (a)

p	1	2	3	4	5
b	3	6	9	12	15

$b = 3p$

(b)

p	1	2	3	4	5
b	4	6	8	10	12

$b = 2p + 2$

(c)

p	1	2	3	4	5
b	4	7	10	13	16

$b = 3p + 1$

Section C (p 10)

1 (a)

Pattern number (p)	1	2	3	4	5
Number of matches (m)	3	6	9	12	15

(b) $m = 3p$

(c)

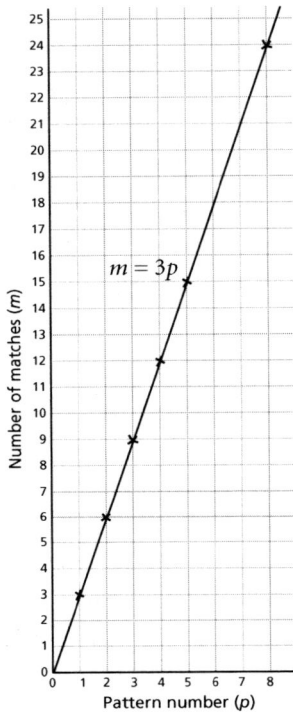

(d) 18

2 (a)

x	1	2	3	4	5
$y = 2x - 1$	1	3	5	7	9

(b) 19

(c), (d)

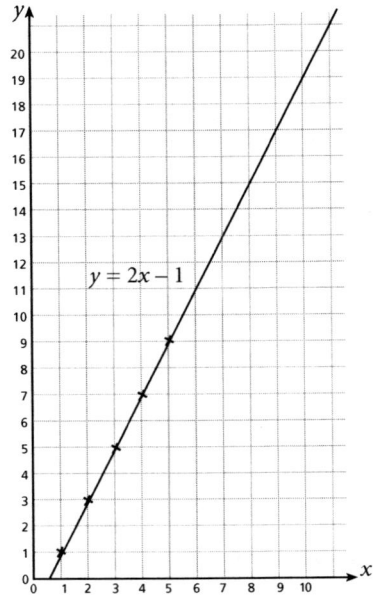

(e) 15

3 (a)

Number of people	5	10	20	30	50
Cost in £	20	30	50	70	110

(b)

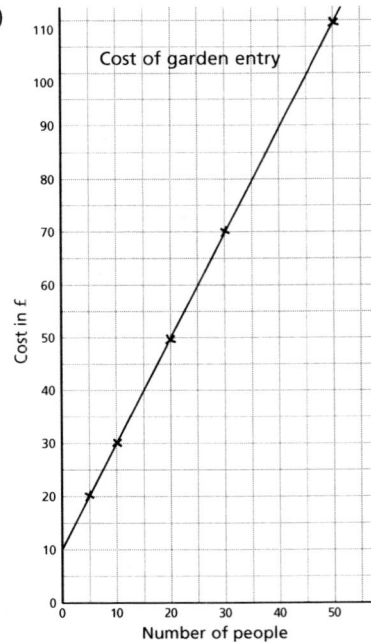

Cost of garden entry

(c) £90

(d) 25 people

⑤ Fractions

Pupils revisit calculating fractions of numbers and are introduced to simplifying fractions and simple addition and subtraction of fractions.

Number bites F1 to F3 on page 6 offer suitable revision for weaker pupils before they start this unit.

> **Practice booklet** pages 12 to 14

Ⓐ **Seeing fractions** (p 29)

This is revision of work done on fractions in earlier SMP Interact material.

◊ The aim of the introduction is to re-establish that the concept of a fraction depends on the equality of parts.

> *'We did this as an interactive question and answer session – it worked well.'*

Ⓑ **Fractions of amounts** (p 30)

This again should be revision of earlier work

◊ Using counters on an OHP is a useful way of demonstrating this concept. The use of such models is also useful later in work on simplifying.

> *'The pupils really liked the questions in this section.'*

Ⓒ **Equivalent fractions** (p 32)

◊ Before pupils open the book, you could start by drawing on the board some pairs of diagrams, similar to those in the book, showing equivalent fractions (e.g. $\frac{4}{6} = \frac{2}{3}$, $\frac{12}{20} = \frac{3}{5}$). By getting pupils to consider and discuss your own questions about your diagrams, pupils may be able to discover for themselves that the top and bottom of the fraction are divided by the same number.

Ⓓ **Adding and subtracting fractions** (p 34)

◊ At this stage pupils are mainly asked to add and subtract fractions with a common denominator, although a few later questions look at simple cases where the denominators are different.

Ⓐ Seeing fractions (p 29)

A1 (a) Red $\frac{2}{5}$, yellow $\frac{3}{5}$

(b) Red $\frac{3}{4}$, yellow $\frac{1}{4}$

(c) Red $\frac{3}{10}$, yellow $\frac{7}{10}$

(d) Red $\frac{5}{8}$, yellow $\frac{3}{8}$

A2 The pupil's drawings of a square with $\frac{3}{4}$ shaded

A3 (a) $\frac{1}{2}$ (b) $\frac{9}{10}$ (c) $\frac{1}{4}$ (d) $\frac{1}{5}$

Ⓑ Fractions of amounts (p 30)

B1 $\frac{1}{4}$ of 20 = 5: B $\frac{1}{10}$ of 30 = 3: C

$\frac{1}{2}$ of 10 = 5: F $\frac{1}{5}$ of 10 = 2: E

$\frac{1}{5}$ of 15 = 3: D $\frac{1}{3}$ of 15 = 5: A

B2 (a) 2 (b) 4 (c) 4 (d) 6

(e) 6 (f) 9 (g) 9 (h) 7

(i) 6 (j) 10 (k) 45 (l) 21

(m) 16 (n) 3 (o) 20

B3 $\frac{3}{4}$ of 16 = 12: C $\frac{2}{3}$ of 15 = 10: E

$\frac{3}{5}$ of 25 = 15: A $\frac{2}{5}$ of 25 = 10: F

$\frac{3}{5}$ of 20 = 12: D $\frac{3}{4}$ of 20 = 15: B

B4 (a) 27 (b) 24 (c) 15 (d) 14

(e) 20 (f) 35 (g) 15 (h) 48

B5 (a) 686 (b) 563 (c) 4238

(d) 4603 (e) 65 437 (f) 3697

B6 18

B7 42 468

B8 60

B9 (a) 148 (b) 255 (c) 4977 (d) 846

B10 9453

B11 769 770

Ⓒ Equivalent fractions (p 32)

C1 $\frac{1}{3} = \frac{2}{6} = \frac{3}{9} = \frac{12}{\mathbf{36}}$

C2 (a) $\frac{1}{5} = \frac{\mathbf{2}}{10}$ (b) $\frac{1}{7} = \frac{2}{\mathbf{14}}$

(c) $\frac{1}{4} = \frac{\mathbf{3}}{12}$ (d) $\frac{1}{2} = \frac{6}{\mathbf{12}}$

(e) $\frac{2}{5} = \frac{\mathbf{6}}{15}$ (f) $\frac{3}{7} = \frac{\mathbf{9}}{21}$

(g) $\frac{5}{12} = \frac{20}{\mathbf{48}}$ (h) $\frac{3}{4} = \frac{\mathbf{18}}{24}$

C3 (a) $\frac{1}{5} = \frac{\mathbf{3}}{15} = \frac{6}{30}$ (b) $\frac{3}{4} = \frac{12}{16} = \frac{15}{20}$

(c) $\frac{2}{3} = \frac{6}{9} = \frac{8}{12} = \frac{14}{\mathbf{21}}$

(d) $\frac{5}{6} = \frac{\mathbf{10}}{12} = \frac{25}{\mathbf{30}} = \frac{\mathbf{15}}{18}$

C4 The pupil's four fractions equivalent to $\frac{3}{5}$

C5 The pupil's four fractions equivalent to $\frac{5}{8}$

C6 The pupil's diagram showing that there are six eighths in $\frac{3}{4}$

C7 The pupil's diagram showing that there are eight twelfths in $\frac{2}{3}$

C8 (a) $\frac{4}{5}$ (b) $\frac{3}{4}$ (c) $\frac{1}{2}$

(d) $\frac{7}{10}$ (e) $\frac{3}{5}$

C9 (a) $\frac{1}{3}$ (b) $\frac{1}{2}$ (c) $\frac{3}{4}$

(d) $\frac{3}{5}$ (e) $\frac{3}{4}$

C10 $\frac{1}{4}$

C11 $\frac{2}{5}$

C12 (a) $\frac{1}{3}$ (b) $\frac{3}{8}$ (c) $\frac{2}{5}$

C13 $\frac{18}{30} = \frac{3}{5}$

C14 (a) $\frac{25}{40} = \frac{5}{8}$ (b) $\frac{10}{40} = \frac{1}{4}$ (c) $\frac{5}{40} = \frac{1}{8}$

C15 (a) $2\frac{1}{4}$ (b) $1\frac{3}{5}$ (c) $1\frac{5}{6}$

(d) $3\frac{1}{4}$ (e) $4\frac{2}{5}$ (f) $2\frac{2}{7}$

(g) $2\frac{3}{10}$ (h) $6\frac{1}{5}$ (i) $5\frac{7}{10}$ (j) $5\frac{1}{4}$

C16 (a) $\frac{5}{2}$ (b) $\frac{11}{3}$ (c) $\frac{17}{5}$ (d) $\frac{17}{7}$

(e) $\frac{19}{5}$ (f) $\frac{27}{8}$ (g) $\frac{16}{3}$ (h) $\frac{38}{5}$

(i) $\frac{38}{9}$ (j) $\frac{73}{12}$

D Adding and subtracting fractions (p 34)

D1 The pupil's diagram to show that $\frac{2}{9} + \frac{5}{9} = \frac{7}{9}$

D2 (a) $\frac{3}{5}$ (b) $\frac{2}{3}$ (c) $\frac{5}{11}$ (d) $\frac{8}{9}$
(e) $\frac{6}{7}$ (f) $\frac{5}{12}$ (g) $\frac{5}{8}$ (h) $\frac{9}{13}$

D3 (a) $\frac{4}{8} = \frac{1}{2}$ (b) $\frac{6}{8} = \frac{3}{4}$ (c) $\frac{8}{12} = \frac{2}{3}$
(d) $\frac{6}{9} = \frac{2}{3}$ (e) $\frac{9}{12} = \frac{3}{4}$ (f) $\frac{6}{12} = \frac{1}{2}$
(g) $\frac{9}{15} = \frac{3}{5}$ (h) $\frac{3}{9} = \frac{1}{3}$

D4 (a) $\frac{5}{9}$ (b) $\frac{1}{3}$ (c) $\frac{4}{11}$ (d) $\frac{4}{9}$
(e) $\frac{3}{8}$ (f) $\frac{5}{12}$ (g) $\frac{1}{8}$ (h) $\frac{1}{9}$

D5 (a) $\frac{1}{2}$ (b) $\frac{1}{3}$ (c) $\frac{1}{2}$ (d) $\frac{1}{2}$
(e) $\frac{1}{4}$ (f) $\frac{5}{6}$ (g) $\frac{1}{4}$ (h) $\frac{3}{8}$

D6 (a) $\frac{1}{2} + \frac{1}{4} = \frac{3}{4}$ (b) $\frac{1}{2} + \frac{1}{8} = \frac{5}{8}$
(c) $\frac{1}{8} + \frac{1}{8} + \frac{1}{8} + \frac{1}{8} = \frac{1}{2}$

D7 (a) $\frac{7}{8}$ (b) $\frac{5}{8}$ (c) $\frac{7}{8}$

*D8 (a) $\frac{3}{4}$ (b) $\frac{3}{4}$ (c) $1\frac{1}{2}$

*D9 (a) $1\frac{1}{8}$ (b) $1\frac{3}{8}$ (c) $2\frac{1}{4}$

What progress have you made? (p 35)

1 (a) 3 (b) 9

2 (a) 30 (b) 21

3 (a) $\frac{2}{5}$ (b) $\frac{7}{10}$

4 (a) $\frac{4}{5}$ (b) $\frac{4}{5}$ (c) $\frac{1}{5}$ (d) $\frac{2}{3}$

5 (a) $\frac{4}{5}$ (b) $\frac{10}{11}$ (c) $\frac{2}{3}$
(d) $\frac{1}{5}$ (e) $\frac{4}{7}$ (f) $\frac{3}{4}$

Practice booklet

Sections A and B (p 12)

1 (a) $\frac{1}{5}$ shaded, $\frac{4}{5}$ unshaded
(b) $\frac{6}{15}$ shaded, $\frac{9}{15}$ unshaded
(c) $\frac{6}{16}$ shaded, $\frac{10}{16}$ unshaded

2 (a) Point marked 7.5 cm from A
(b) Point marked 4 cm from A

3 (a) The pupil's diagram with 3 parts shaded.
(b) 3

4 (a) 8 (b) 7 (c) 6 (d) 8
(e) 12 (f) 6 (g) 14 (h) 25

5 25

6 195

7 (a) 300 (b) 180 (c) 126 (d) 440

Section C (p 13)

1 $\frac{1}{5} = \frac{\mathbf{2}}{\mathbf{10}} = \frac{3}{\mathbf{15}} = \frac{\mathbf{4}}{20}$

2 (a) $\frac{1}{10} = \frac{\mathbf{2}}{20}$ (b) $\frac{1}{8} = \frac{2}{\mathbf{16}}$
(c) $\frac{1}{6} = \frac{\mathbf{4}}{24}$ (d) $\frac{1}{3} = \frac{5}{15}$
(e) $\frac{3}{4} = \frac{\mathbf{9}}{12}$ (f) $\frac{2}{5} = \frac{20}{\mathbf{50}}$
(g) $\frac{5}{9} = \frac{\mathbf{20}}{36}$ (h) $\frac{3}{10} = \frac{18}{\mathbf{60}}$

3 The pupil's four fractions equivalent to $\frac{2}{3}$

4 (a) $\frac{1}{2}$ (b) $\frac{1}{4}$ (c) $\frac{2}{5}$ (d) $\frac{2}{3}$

5 $\frac{2}{3}$

6 (a) $\frac{1}{2}$ (b) $\frac{2}{3}$ (c) $\frac{3}{5}$ (d) $\frac{3}{4}$

7 $\frac{3}{5}$

8 (a) $\frac{1}{2}$ (b) $\frac{3}{10}$ (c) $\frac{1}{5}$

Section D (p 14)

1 $\frac{3}{11} + \frac{4}{11} = \frac{\mathbf{7}}{\mathbf{11}}$

2 (a) $\frac{3}{5}$ (b) $\frac{7}{12}$ (c) $\frac{3}{4}$ (d) $\frac{1}{4}$

3 (a) $\frac{2}{3}$ (b) $\frac{2}{7}$ (c) $\frac{3}{5}$ (d) $\frac{3}{5}$

4 (a) $\frac{1}{3} + \frac{1}{6} = \frac{1}{2}$ (b) $\frac{2}{3} + \frac{1}{6} = \frac{5}{6}$
(c) $\frac{1}{4} + \frac{3}{8} = \frac{5}{8}$

*5 (a) $\frac{5}{8}$ (b) $\frac{3}{8}$ (c) $\frac{5}{8}$

Review 1 (p 36)

1 (a) £4.66   (b) £1.95
  (c) £1.72   (d) 25p
  (e) 0.5 kg bag costs £3.30 per kilogram,
      1 kg bag costs £2.99 per kilogram,
      2.5 kg bag costs £2.20 per kilogram,
      so the 2.5 kg bag is cheaper per
      kilogram.

2 (a) 6852   (b) 936

3 $\frac{20}{32} = \frac{5}{8}$

4 (a) An (isosceles) right-angled triangle
  (b) An isosceles triangle
  (c) The pupil's numbers to give a
      triangle congruent to 2, 5, 7
  (d) A trapezium
  (e) A kite

5 (a) $1\frac{3}{4}$ (b) $2\frac{1}{6}$ (c) $3\frac{2}{5}$ (d) $4\frac{1}{2}$

6 (a)

Pattern number (p)	1	2	3	4	5
Number of matches (m)	4	6	8	10	12

  (b) $m = 2p + 2$ (c) 22

(d), (e)

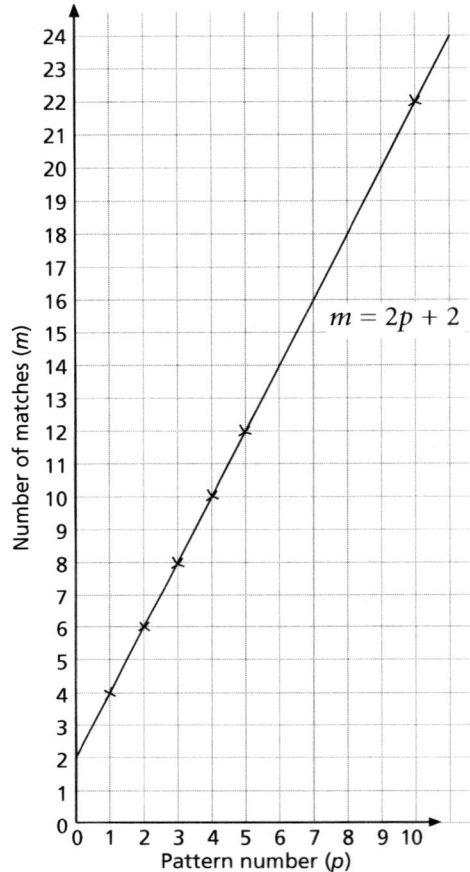

(f) Pattern 8

7 (a) $\frac{1}{4}$ (b) $\frac{3}{4}$

8 (a) $\frac{8}{11}$ (b) $\frac{7}{9}$ (c) $\frac{3}{8}$ (d) $\frac{1}{6}$

Mixed questions 1 (Practice booklet p 15)

1 (a) £1.70   (b) £21

2 (a) 1 litre pack £0.50 per litre
      4 litre pack £0.40 per litre
      6 litre pack £0.44 per litre

  (b) 4 litre pack

3 A $m = 3p$; B $m = 3p + 1$; C $m = 4p$

4 (a) $\frac{5}{7}$ (b) $\frac{1}{6}$ (c) $\frac{2}{3}$ (d) $\frac{1}{2}$

⑥ Probability

This unit uses fractions to express probabilities and invites pupils to compare probabilities for different events using fractions. The idea of equivalent fractions is also met in this unit.

p 38	**A** Your choice!	Games requiring pupils to make judgements about relative probabilities
p 40	**B** Using fractions	Stating a probability in a variety of situations
p 42	**C** Comparing fractions	Use to compare probabilities

Essential	**Optional**
Sets of cards numbered 1–9 (one set per pair) or cards from an ordinary pack of playing cards Sheet 269	Paper cups and marbles OHP transparency of sheet 269

Practice booklet pages 16 to 18 (needs sheet 269)

𝔸 **Your choice!** (p 38)

Pupils may not have a common understanding of the everyday language of probability; the initial games are designed to clarify this. The game 'Higher or lower' encourages pupils to make relative probability judgements based on the number of possible outcomes.

Sets of cards numbered 1–9 (one set per pair) or cards from an ordinary pack of playing cards

'I played against the whole class first.'

'Both games worked extremely well.'

◊ In the game 'Up or down' pupils should be encouraged to use terms such as 'more likely', 'less likely', 'certain' and 'impossible'. The use of fractions is not required at this stage but pupils should give reasons for their choices. The game could initially (at least) be played as a class activity. It could be played with an ordinary dice, but this gives no occasion when there is the same chance for each choice.

◊ The game 'Higher or lower' can initially be played on the board with the teacher as compere. By writing down the numbers 1 to 9, circling the current last number and crossing out all the previously shown cards, pupils will be able to count how many of cards are higher or lower. It is useful to discuss situations where you are guaranteed to win a point.

B Using fractions (p 40)

This section involves writing probability more formally as a fraction.

> Optional: Paper cups and marbles

'They liked the "Find the marble" games.'

◊ Some pupils may need to see real cups and marbles to understand the described situation. By using different numbers of cups and marbles the ideas of relative probability could be extended from the previous section.

◊ A common mistake where there are, say, 2 black and 3 white counters in a bag is for pupils to write the probability of drawing black as $\frac{2}{3}$. Questions from B4 onwards emphasise the need to use the total number of outcomes as the denominator in probability fractions.

C Comparing fractions (p 42)

In this section pupils first compare fractions by shading. Then they use this to compare probabilities.

> Sheet 269
> Optional: OHP transparency of sheet 269

◊ On sheet 269, each rectangular strip has 12 parts. By shading these strips, pupils can compare some simple fractions. Pupils have shaded rectangles to compare fractions before. The first example in the introduction simply revises this.

In the second example, ensure that pupils know how to shade $\frac{3}{4}$ of the rectangular strip. It may help if they first mark each of the quarters on the strip, and then shade 3 of these. Similarly to shade $\frac{5}{6}$, they may wish first to mark each of the sixths on the strip and then shade 5 of these.

More confident pupils may be able to use the work on equivalent fractions in the preceding unit on fractions to help with later questions in this section.

Practice booklet (p 16)

> Sheet 269 (for section C)

A Your choice! (p 38)

A1 (a) Lower (b) Higher (c) Lower

A2 (a) 1 or 5 (b) 3

A3 (a) Lower (b) Higher (c) Lower
 (d) Lower (e) Either

A4 A (A has 1 out of 4 higher, B has 1 out of 6 higher and C has 1 out of 5 higher.)

B Using fractions (p 40)

B1 (a) $\frac{2}{5}$ (b) $\frac{2}{3}$ (c) $\frac{3}{5}$ (c) $\frac{3}{4}$

B2 (a) $\frac{1}{2}$ (b) $\frac{2}{4}$ (c) $\frac{3}{6}$

B3 They are all the same probability.

B4 (a) $\frac{4}{8}$ or $\frac{1}{2}$ (b) $\frac{3}{8}$ (c) $\frac{5}{8}$

  (d) $\frac{2}{8}$ or $\frac{1}{4}$

B5 (a) $\frac{6}{10}$ or $\frac{3}{5}$ (b) $\frac{4}{10}$ or $\frac{2}{5}$

B6 (a) $\frac{7}{12}$ (b) $\frac{5}{12}$ (c) One that works

B7 (a) 5 (b) $\frac{3}{5}$ (c) $\frac{2}{5}$

B8 (a) 12 (b) $\frac{6}{12}$ or $\frac{1}{2}$ (c) $\frac{4}{12}$ or $\frac{1}{3}$

  (d) $\frac{2}{12}$ or $\frac{1}{6}$

B9 (a) 28 (b) $\frac{12}{28}$ or $\frac{3}{7}$ (c) $\frac{16}{28}$ or $\frac{4}{7}$

B10 (a) $\frac{5}{10}$ or $\frac{1}{2}$ (b) $\frac{3}{10}$ (c) $\frac{2}{10}$ or $\frac{1}{5}$

  (d) S stands for yellow, T stands for blue and U stands for red.

ℂ Comparing fractions (p 42)

C1 (a) ▭
  (b) ▭
  (c) $\frac{3}{4}$

C2 (a) $\frac{7}{12}$ is greater than $\frac{1}{2}$ (with the pupil's shaded fraction boxes).

  (b) $\frac{5}{6}$ is greater than $\frac{9}{12}$ (with the pupil's shaded fraction boxes).

  (c) $\frac{8}{12}$ is the same as $\frac{2}{3}$ (with the pupil's shaded fraction boxes).

C3 $\frac{1}{6}, \frac{1}{4}, \frac{4}{12}$ (with shaded boxes)

C4 The chance is the same (with the pupil's explanation).

C5 $\frac{4}{6}$ and $\frac{8}{12}$ (with shaded boxes)

C6 Two of

C7 (a) A: $\frac{2}{6}$ or $\frac{1}{3}$ B: $\frac{1}{4}$; A greater
  (b) A: $\frac{4}{6}$ or $\frac{2}{3}$ B: $\frac{2}{3}$; same
  (c) A: $\frac{3}{4}$ B: $\frac{2}{3}$; A greater
  (d) A: $\frac{3}{6}$ or $\frac{1}{2}$ B: $\frac{1}{2}$; same

C8 (a) Bag 2 gives the greater chance.
  (b) Bag 2 gives the greater chance.

  (c) Both bags give the same chance.
  (d) Bag 2 gives the greater chance.

C9 (a) Box X (b) Box Q (c) Box N

What progress have you made? (p 44)

1 (a) Lower (b) Higher
  (c) The same chance

2 (a) $\frac{2}{5}$ (b) $\frac{5}{7}$ (c) $\frac{7}{12}$

3 Bag F

4 Box B

Practice booklet

Section A (p 16)

1 The 'best guesses' are
  (a) Lower (b) Higher (c) Higher

2 1 or 8

3 Before

4 After

5 (a) Before (b) After (c) Before

6 (a) Before (b) After (c) Before

Section B (p 17)

1 (a) $\frac{1}{5}$ (b) $\frac{2}{3}$ (c) $\frac{3}{7}$

2 (a) 15 (b) $\frac{8}{15}$ (c) $\frac{7}{15}$

3 (a) 28 (b) $\frac{11}{28}$ (c) $\frac{17}{28}$

4 (a) 20 pens (b) $\frac{10}{20}$ or $\frac{1}{2}$ (c) $\frac{6}{20}$ or $\frac{3}{10}$
  (d) $\frac{4}{20}$ or $\frac{1}{5}$

5 (a) 10 packets of crisps (b) $\frac{3}{10}$
  (c) $\frac{6}{10}$ or $\frac{3}{5}$

Section C (p 18)

1 (a) $\frac{8}{12}$ is larger (and the pupil's shading)
  (b) $\frac{2}{3}$ is larger (and the pupil's shading)
  (c) $\frac{1}{4}$ is larger (and the pupil's shading)

2 (a) $\frac{7}{12}, \frac{3}{4}, \frac{5}{6}$ (b) $\frac{1}{6}, \frac{1}{4}, \frac{1}{3}$

3 (a) Game A (b) Game B (c) Game A

7 Earning money (p 45)

This unit gives practice in dividing and multiplying by decimals.

Essential
Calculators
Practice booklet page 19

'I used some wage slips to show them examples – next year some will have part-time jobs.'

◊ Use the introduction to ask how much each of these jobs pays for one hour. You will need to ensure that a number of topics are raised.

- Abbreviations used in advertisements, among others: p/h or ph (per hour), p/a or pa (per annum, i.e. per year), hpw (hours per week).
- A job paying, for example, £20 000 per year can be considered as paying £(20 000 ÷ 52) per week, as the year will have to include paid holidays.

◊ Interest in the topic will be increased if the class has access to local newspapers and pupils compare the rates of pay offered by different job advertisements. You may well come across further abbreviations that will need investigating!

◊ In the introduction, the rates of pay per hour are:
College of Technology… £5.75, Cleaner Tues…£5.55, Morning cleaner… £5.85, Full-time cleaner… £5.75

1 £186.20

2 £6.50

3 (a) £255 (b) £165.60 (c) £65.64

4 £4.81

5 (a) £5.50 (b) £4.85 (c) £4.36

6 (a) £243.19 (b) £6.49

7
	Weekly earnings	Hourly rate
(a)	£105.77	£5.72
(b)	£315.27	£8.59
(c)	£257.69	£7.02
(d)	£570.40	£15.42
(e)	£231.92	£10.31

8 Job B (switchboard operator) had the best hourly rate of £5.76. (The rates for A and C are £5.66 and £5.60.)

Practice booklet (p 19)

1 (a) £198.80 (b) £5.40

2 (a) £59.80 (b) £239.40 (c) £126.00

3 (a) £6.30 (b) £5.32 (c) £5.99

4 (a) £6.35 (b) £5.36 (c) £5.78
   (d) £6.32 (e) £7.58 (f) £6.39

8 Garden centre (p 47)

This is another opportunity to practise mental arithmetic or quick paper and pencil methods.

◊ Introduce the picture by asking simple questions about it. For example:
  • How many plants are in the tray of primulas? (12)
  • How much does hazel hedging grow each year? (70 cm)
  • How many different sizes of clay pot are for sale? (5)
  • What area will one roll of lawn turf cover? ($2 \, m^2$)

◊ A few questions are given below. These are just examples of the types of questions you might ask.

Adding

1 What does one primula and one marigold cost? (£1.40)

2 How many litres of compost are there in one bag of potting compost and one bag of peat-free compost in total? (200 litres)

3 How much do I have to pay for a large clay pot and a bag of peat-free compost? (£14.49)

4 I buy one pot for £3.25 and another for £8.50. How much is that? (£11.75)

5 What would one bag of potting compost and one bag of peat-free compost cost altogether? (£9.48)

Subtracting

1 How much more is one primula than one viola? (30p)

2 How much more does a hazel hedge grow than a box hedge in one year? (40 cm)

3 How many litres more do you get in a bag of potting compost than a bag of seed compost? (40 litres)

4 What is the difference in price of a small pot and a medium pot? (£3.75)

5 How much cheaper is a bag of seed compost than a bag of peat-free compost? (50p)

Multiplying

1 How many plants are there in 4 trays of primulas? (48)

2 What do I have to pay for 3 leylandii? (£13.50)

3 What do 4 primulas cost? (£3.20)

4 How many centimetres does a hazel hedge grow in 3 years? (210 cm = 2.1 m)

5 How much are 6 rolls of lawn turf? (£24)

Dividing

1 If I buy 10 leylandii, how much does each one cost? (£4)

2 How many 20 litre tubs could I fill with one bag of potting compost? (6)

3 How many years does it take a holly hedge to grow 80 cm? (4 years)

4 How many medium size pots could I buy for £50? (7)

5 How many rolls of lawn turf would you need for a lawn whose area is 18 m^2? (9)

Combinations of operations

1 What would 160 litres of seed compost cost? (£5.98)

2 What is the cost of 4 primula and 5 marigold plants? (£6.20)

3 How much do you save by buying a tray of primula plants rather than buying 12 individually? (£1.60)

4 A box hedging plant is 50 cm tall when it is bought. How tall will it be after 3 years? (140 cm = 1.4 m)

5 How many bags of seed compost contain the same amount in litres as two bags of potting compost? (3)

6 What is the least you would have to pay for 12 leylandii? (£49)

7 How much would 240 litres of potting compost cost? (£11.98)

8 What is the cost of 2 small pots and 3 large ones? (£39.50)

9 What would it cost to buy turf to make a 16 square metre lawn? (£32)

10 How many rolls of turf would you need for a lawn which measures 5 m by 6 m? (15)

⑨ Percentages

Pupils should work through this unit without a calculator.

p 48	**A**	50 per cent	Revision of the equivalence of 50% and $\frac{1}{2}$
p 49	**B**	25 per cent	Revision of the equivalence of 25% and $\frac{1}{4}$
p 50	**C**	75 per cent	Finding 75% as a fraction or as 3 lots of 25%
p 51	**D**	10 per cent	From 10% (tenths) to multiples of 10%
p 52	**E**	5 per cent	From 10% to 5%, then to multiples of 10% with 5%

Practice booklet pages 20 to 22

Ⓐ **50 per cent** (p 48)

◊ The 'True or false' statements in the lower box are for discussion.

◊ You may also wish to do A1 and A2 orally.

'We also looked at percentages in newspapers and on food.'

Ⓑ **25 per cent** (p 49)

◊ After revising the fact that 25% is equivalent to $\frac{1}{4}$, discuss different ways of finding 25%, for example halving and then halving again.

◊ The 'True or false' statements are again for discussion.

◊ Use the 'Working backwards' examples as the basis for discussion, perhaps in groups and then by the whole class. There are several equally valid ways of solving these simple problems, and discussing different ways will help extend pupils' understanding.

Ⓒ **75 per cent** (p 50)

◊ Use the introduction to discuss the different ways that 75% can be found. Then broaden the discussion to solving problems of the types set in questions C7 and C9.

D **10 per cent** (p 51)

◊ Ensure that pupils understand that 10% is the same as $\frac{1}{10}$, and therefore 10% can be found by dividing by 10. Include discussion of problems like D8 in your introduction.

E **5 per cent** (p 52)

◊ Pupils should understand that 5% is half of 10%. So, to find 5%, divide by 10 then halve.

You might ask some pupils to work out $17\frac{1}{2}$% VAT by breaking it down into 10% plus 5% plus half of 5%.

A **50 per cent** (p 48)

A1 (a) 4   (b) 9   (c) 100
    (d) 23   (e) 240   (f) 4.5

A2 (a) £3   (b) £3.50   (c) 25 cm
    (d) 220 g   (e) 1.5 m   (f) £70

A3 A and D

A4 (a) 7   (b) £5   (c) 20 cm
    (d) 150   (e) £25   (f) 16p
    (g) £3.02   (h) 54   (i) 2.5 m
    (j) £7.50   (k) 106 cm   (l) 330 g

B **25 per cent** (p 49)

B1 B and C

B2 (a) 4   (b) 10   (c) 3 m
    (d) 50 g   (e) £60   (f) £2.50

B3 £150

B4 (a) £400   (b) £200   (c) £200

B5 £120

B6 32

B7 28

C **75 per cent** (p 50)

C1 A and C

C2 (a) 15   (b) £3   (c) £75
    (d) 9 m   (e) 6 kg   (f) £1.20

C3 600 g

C4 135 cm

C5 (a) 18   (b) 6

C6 2250 litres

C7 12

C8 (a) 9   (b) 30   (c) 36
    (d) 60   (e) 450   (f) 1.5

C9 18

C10 (a) 27   (b) 36   (c) 150
    (d) 15   (e) 180   (f) 1.5

*C11 1200 grams

D **10 per cent** (p 51)

D1 (a) 3   (b) £7   (c) 12 cm
    (d) 5 kg   (e) 70   (f) £15

D2 (a) £1   (b) £0.90 or 90p
    (c) £0.50 or 50p   (d) 0.5 m
    (e) £7.50   (f) 6.5 kg

D3 (a) 3   (b) 6   (c) 16   (d) 28

D4 (a) 6   (b) 14   (c) £4
(d) 16p   (e) 24   (f) 62 g

D5 (a) 12   (b) 18
(c) 33   (d) 27p
(e) £0.30 or 30p   (f) 60 km

D6 (a) 16   (b) 24p   (c) £320
(d) 96 km   (e) £2.16

D7 £3000

D8 450 grams

D9 Alice £120; Charlie £360; Harry £480

D10 21 km

E **5 per cent** (p 52)

E1 (a) $1\frac{1}{2}$ (b) £6   (c) £23
(d) 4 km   (e) 25 g

E2 (a) 3   (b) £21   (c) £48
(d) 13.5 km   (e) £7.50

E3 (a) 27   (b) £9   (c) £13.50
(d) 72 m   (e) 900 kg

E4 (a) 52   (b) £78   (c) £169
(d) 32.5 g   (e) £45.50

E5 (a) £22   (b) £33   (c) £495
(d) 143 m   (e) £5.50

E6 (a) 19p   (b) £57   (c) 47.5 g
(d) £2850   (e) £4.75

E7 Son £10 000;   daughter £10 000;
grandchildren £7500 each

E8 270

E9 126

E10 800

E11 £1200

Fraction percentage puzzle

PLUM

What progress have you made? (p 53)

1 (a) £8.50   (b) 12 m

2 (a) 63   (b) £13   (c) 7.5 g

3 (a) 36   (b) £3.50

4 (a) £12   (b) 78 m

5 (a) $\frac{1}{2}$ (b) $\frac{3}{4}$

Practice booklet

Sections A and B (p 20)

1 A: 25%   B: neither
C: 50%   D: neither

2 (a) 12 kg   (b) 20 cm   (c) 9 litres
(d) 24 mm   (e) 2.5 m

3 (a) 10 kg   (b) 5 cm   (c) 6 litres
(d) 15 mm   (e) 2 m

4 (a) 400 g   (b) 200 g

5 (a) 8   (b) 16

6 (a) 12 km   (b) 6 km   (c) 6 km

7 32 pupils

Section C (p 21)

1 C

2 (a) 12 kg   (b) 150 m   (c) 60 litres
(d) £7.50   (e) 22.5 mm

3 1500 metres

4 (a) 900   (b) 300

5 $\frac{3}{4}$

6 (a) 300 g   (b) 180 g   (c) 225 g

*7 80 years old

*8 (a) 200 cm   (b) 160 cm   (c) 176 cm

Sections D and E (p 22)

1 (a) 20 g (b) 15 mm (c) £18
   (d) 6 kg (e) £0.80 or 80p

2 They are both the same, 50p.

3 (a) £6 (b) £3 (c) £9 (d) £21

4 (a) 12 kg (b) 6 mm (c) 18 g
   (d) 36 m (e) 21 litres

5 (a) £4 (b) £44 (c) £76 (d) £36

6 (a) £30 (b) £16 (c) £48
   (d) £64 (e) £180

7 (a) 30 g carbohydrate, 12 g fat
       and 18 g protein
   (b) 37.5 g carbohydrate, 15 g fat
       and 22.5 g protein

8 About 78 pupils

*9 (a) 140 fish (b) 39 fish (c) 221 fish

⑩ Square deal

Pupils solve hollow number grid problems using addition and subtraction.
This includes using the idea of an inverse operation ('working backwards').

Algebra arises in the context of these grids. Pupils simplify
expressions such as $n + 4 + n - 3$.

p 54	**A** Hollow grids	Simple addition and subtraction problems
		Investigating simple general rules on hollow grids
p 57	**B** Using algebra	Expressing in algebra that, for example, a number 3 more than n is $n + 3$
		Simplifying expressions such as $n - 6 + 1$
p 59	**C** Opposite corners	Simplifying expressions such as $n + 4 + n - 3$
		Using algebra to show that a simple statement is true

> **Optional**
> Sheets 270, 271, 272
>
> **Practice booklet** pages 23 to 26

Ⓐ **Hollow grids** (p 54)

This section leads into the algebra in section B.

> Optional:
> Sheet 270 (for recording answers to A1 and A2)
> Sheet 271 (blank grids for A3 and A4)

◊ Point out that the operations used on these grids are restricted to addition and subtraction. Emphasise that the 'across' rule applies to *both rows* and the 'down' rule applies to *both columns*.

'A good approach for this level of ability. Drawing the grids was good practice for their drawing skills.'

You could choose two pupils to complete a grid. One could start going across and the other going down. Either route will give the same result for the bottom right square and pupils could try to explain why this is the case.

You may wish to ensure that the numbers in the the top left square are large enough to avoid the complication of negative numbers. Negative numbers do not occur in any grid in the unit.

Questions can be posed in a class discussion, for example:

- Suppose the number in this square is 20 (indicating a square).
  What number will be in this square (indicating another square)?
- What happens if the 'across' and 'down' rules change places?

Ask pupils to explain how they worked out their answers. You could introduce the idea of an 'inverse' and encourage more confident pupils to use this word in their explanations.

A3 Negative numbers appear in the grid if pupils choose 0 or 1 for the top left number, providing an opportunity to consolidate work on negative numbers. However, if you want to avoid this, you could suggest that pupils choose numbers greater than 1 for the top left square.

In part (f), encourage pupils to use their rule from part (e), rather than completing the grids.

A4 Pupils can extend this and investigate for their own pairs of rules.

In one school, a spreadsheet was set up for hollow grids. For A1 and A2 pupils tried the problems one by one and, after each problem, the teacher used the spreadsheet to quickly find the solution. Pupils checked their work before moving on to the next grid. This kept things moving and pupils enjoyed the immediate feedback.

B **Using algebra** (p 57)

Pupils often find it difficult to simplify expressions that involve subtraction. To start with, you may wish to restrict the rules to addition only. This allows a more gradual introduction of the main ideas.

Optional: Sheet 271 (for recording answers to B1 and B4)

◊ You may find a number line is helpful in getting these ideas across.

◊ Remind pupils of earlier work in A3 and A4 on finding rules. Emphasise that the expressions in the completed grid show immediately how to find any number in any position on the grid from the top left number.

◊ In the first grid, pupils who think that '$n - 7$' should be in the square to the right of '$n - 3$' are possibly thinking of '$n - 3 + 4$' as '$n - (3 + 4)$'. Discussion of numerical examples as shown with the help of a number line should help to clear up any confusion.

◊ Encourage pupils to use both routes to find the expression in the bottom right square to check their work.

ℂ **Opposite corners** (p 59)

Pupils begin with an investigation (which can be quite short) that leads into the algebra. The emphasis is on showing that the opposite corners totals are the same each time. Before pupils work on this section, they need to be confident in simplifying expressions.

> Optional:
> Sheet 271 (for recording answers to C4(a))
> Sheet 272 (blank 3 by 3 grids)

Investigation

◊ You could start by showing the pupils a 3 by 3 hollow grid with, say, '+ 2' and '+ 5' as the rules. Pupils can choose their own top left numbers and fill in the grid. Now ask them to add the pairs of numbers in the opposite corners. Each pupil should find that their totals are equal.

You could record some of the results in a table. Some pupils may see that the rule to find the total is 'multiply the top left number by 2 and then add 14'.

◊ Pupils can investigate adding opposite corners on grids of their own. They should find that the totals of the opposite corners are the same, irrespective of the rules used or the size of the grid.

◊ The investigation into opposite corners leads into discussion of the algebra at the top of page 58.

Make sure pupils grasp that
* $n + n = 2 \times n = 2n$ (they may find '2 lots of n' simpler than '$2 \times n$')
* $n + n + 6 = 2n + 6$ for any value of n.
So $n + n + 6$ and $2n + 6$ are called **equivalent expressions**.

◊ Some pupils may see that you have also found a rule to work out the total, in this case $2n + 6$. So if a grid like this has, say, 50 in the top left square, then the opposite corners total will be $(2 \times 50) + 6 = 106$.

To check this result, pupils could complete the grid and find the opposite corners total.

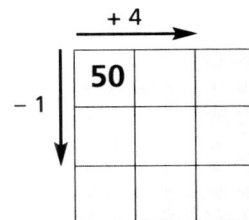

A Hollow grids (p 54)

A1 (a) $+2$ →, $+5$ ↓

1	3	5
6		10
11	13	15

(b) -3 →, $+1$ ↓

11	8	5	2
12			3
13			4
14	11	8	5

(c) $+3$ →, $+4$ ↓

2	5	8
6		12
10	13	16

(d) $+4$ →, -2 ↓

20	24	28	32	36
18				34
16				32
14				30
12	16	20	24	28

(e) -3 →, -1 ↓

15	12	9	6
14			5
13			4
12	9	6	3

A2 (a) $+4$ →, $+5$ ↓

2	6	10
7		15
12	16	20

(b) -2 →, $+3$ ↓

8	6	4
11		7
14	12	10

(c) $+3$ →, -1 ↓

5	8	11	14
4			13
3			12
2	5	8	11

(d) $+3$ →, -2 ↓

12	15	18
10		16
8	11	14

(e) $+5$ →, -2 ↓

7	12	17	22
5			20
3			18
1	6	11	16

(f) $+5$ →, $+3$ ↓

1	6	11
4		14
7	12	17

(g) -4 →, -1 ↓

19	15	11
18		10
17	13	9

(h) $+2$ →, $+5$ ↓

1	3	5
6		11
13	15	17

(i) $+1$ →, $+2$ ↓

10	11	12	13
12			15
14			17
16	17	18	19

(j) -3 →, $+6$ ↓

13	10	7
19		13
25	22	19

(k) -5 →, -4 ↓

20	15	10
16		6
12	7	2

(l) -6 →, -2 ↓

24	18	12	6
22			4
20			2
18	12	6	0

A3 (a) $+3$ →, -1 ↓

3	6	9
2		8
1	4	7

$+3$ →, -1 ↓

20	23	26
19		25
18	21	24

$+3$ →, -1 ↓

100	103	106
99		105
98	101	104

(b)

Top left number	Bottom right number
3	7
20	**24**
100	**104**

(c) The pupil's grids

(d) The pupil's results

(e) The pupil's description of the rule, for example, 'Add 4 to the top left number to find the bottom right.'

(f) (i) 46   (ii) 134

A4 (a) The pupil's grids

(b) The pupil's table

(c) The pupil's description of the rule, for example, 'Take 2 from the top left number to find the bottom right.'

(d) 98

B Using algebra (p 57)

B1 (a)

→ + 7

↓ + 1

n	$n+7$	$n+14$
$n+1$		$n+15$
$n+2$	$n+9$	$n+16$

(b)

→ + 5

↓ − 3

a	$a+5$	$a+10$	$a+15$
$a-3$			$a+12$
$a-6$			$a+9$
$a-9$	$a-4$	$a+1$	$a+6$

(c)

→ − 4

↓ + 2

k	$k-4$	$k-8$
$k+2$		$k-6$
$k+4$	k	$k-4$

(d)

→ − 1

↓ − 3

b	$b-1$	$b-2$	$b-3$
$b-3$			$b-6$
$b-6$			$b-9$
$b-9$	$b-10$	$b-11$	$b-12$

(e)

→ − 2

↓ + 8

h	$h-2$	$h-4$
$h+8$		$h+4$
$h+16$	$h+14$	$h+12$

(f)

→ + 3

↓ − 7

g	$g+3$	$g+6$	$g+9$
$g-7$			$g+2$
$g-14$			$g-5$
$g-21$	$g-18$	$g-15$	$g-12$

B2 (a) 116 (b) 106 (c) 96
(d) 88 (e) 112 (f) 88

B3 (a) $f+11$ (b) $y+12$ (c) $x+15$
(d) $z+3$ (e) $p+3$ (f) $m-7$
(g) $q-7$ (h) $w-5$ (i) $h+8$
(j) $a+8$ (k) $b-9$ (l) $c-4$
(m) $d-10$ (n) e (o) $g-12$

*B4 (a)

→ + 4

↓ + 2

p	$p+4$	$p+8$
$p+2$		$p+10$
$p+4$	$p+8$	$p+12$

(b)

→ + 4

↓ − 3

x	$x+4$	$x+8$
$x-3$		$x+5$
$x-6$	$x-2$	$x+2$

(c)

$-1 \rightarrow$
$-6 \downarrow$

y	$y-1$	$y-2$
$y-6$		$y-8$
$y-12$	$y-13$	$y-14$

ℂ Opposite corners (p 59)

C1 (a)

$+3 \rightarrow$
$+2 \downarrow$

20	23	26
22		28
24	27	30

(b) (i) 50   (ii) 50

(c) Yes

C2 (a)

$+3 \rightarrow$
$+2 \downarrow$

p	$p+3$	$p+6$
$p+2$		$p+8$
$p+4$	$p+7$	$p+10$

(b) Both pairs add up to $2p + 10$.

(c) Yes

(d) (i) 210   (ii) 210

C3 A and D $(2n + 7)$ B and I $(2n - 9)$
C and G $(2n - 5)$ E and H $(2n - 11)$

C4 Grid P

(a)

$+4 \rightarrow$
$-2 \downarrow$

p	$p+4$	$p+8$
$p-2$		$p+6$
$p-4$	p	$p+4$

(b) Both pairs add to give $2p + 4$.

(c) Yes

Grid Q

(a)

$-3 \rightarrow$
$+1 \downarrow$

q	$q-3$	$q-6$
$q+1$		$q-5$
$q+2$	$q-1$	$q-4$

(b) Both pairs add to give $2q - 4$.

(c) Yes

Grid R

(a)

$-4 \rightarrow$
$+5 \downarrow$

r	$r-4$	$r-8$	$r-12$
$r+5$			$r-7$
$r+10$			$r-2$
$r+15$	$r+11$	$r+7$	$r+3$

(b) Both pairs add to give $2r + 3$.

(c) Yes

Grid S

(a)

$+2 \rightarrow$
$-5 \downarrow$

s	$s+2$	$s+4$	$s+6$
$s-5$			$s+1$
$s-10$			$s-4$
$s-15$	$s-13$	$s-11$	$s-9$

(b) Both pairs add to give $2s - 9$.

(c) Yes

Grid T

(a)

Grid with arrow −3 across top, −4 down left:

t	t−3	t−6
t−4		t−10
t−8	t−11	t−14

(b) Both pairs add to give $2t - 14$.

(c) Yes

C5 (a) $2n + 10$ (b) $2m + 5$ (c) $3k + 5$
(d) $2j + 2$ (e) $2h - 5$ (f) $3g + 4$
(g) $3f + 4$ (h) $2e - 9$ (i) $2d - 5$
(j) $2c - 10$ (k) $2b - 8$ (l) $4a + 2$

What progress have you made? (p 61)

1 (a) arrow −1 across, +3 down:

4	3	2
7		5
10	9	8

(b) arrow +5 across, −3 down:

10	15	20
7		17
4	9	14

2 (a) Across: + 4
(b) Across: − 2
Down: − 4

3 (a) +5 across, −1 down:

t	t+5	t+10
t−1		t+9
t−2	t+3	t+8

(b) −4 across, +1 down:

t	t−4	t−8
t+1		t−7
t+2	t−2	t−6

(c) −3 across, −2 down:

t	t−3	t−6
t−2		t−8
t−4	t−7	t−10

4 (a) $k + 1$ (b) $j - 6$ (c) $h - 10$
(d) $2g + 5$ (e) $2f - 2$ (f) $3e - 4$
(g) $3d$ (h) $3c - 1$

Practice booklet

Section A (p 23)

1 (a) +4 across, +5 down:

3	7	11
8		16
13	17	21

(b) +6 across, −4 down:

19	25	31	37	43
15				39
11				35
7				31
3	9	15	21	27

(c) −1 across, +3 down:

12	11	10	9
15			12
18			15
21	20	19	18

(d) −3 across, −2 down:

20	17	14	11
18			9
16			7
14	11	8	5

2 (a) +3 across, −2 down:

10	13	16
8		14
6	9	12

(b) −3 across, +5 down:

8	5	2
13		7
18	15	12

(c) −4 across, −5 down:

20	16	12
15		7
10	6	2

3 (a) $+6 \rightarrow$ $-3 \downarrow$

9	15	21	27
6			24
3			21
0	6	12	18

(b) $-2 \rightarrow$ $-3 \downarrow$

16	14	12	10
13			7
10			4
7	5	3	1

(c) $+3 \rightarrow$ $+5 \downarrow$

3	6	9	12
8			17
13			22
18	21	24	27

4 (a) The pupil's grids

(b) The pupil's table

(c) Add 2 to the top left number to find the bottom right.

(d) 52

Section B (p 25)

1 (a) $+5 \rightarrow$ $+2 \downarrow$

n	$n+5$	$n+10$
$n+2$		$n+12$
$n+4$	$n+9$	$n+14$

(b) $+6 \rightarrow$ $-2 \downarrow$

m	$m+6$	$m+12$	$m+18$
$m-2$			$m+16$
$m-4$			$m+14$
$m-6$	m	$m+6$	$m+12$

(c) $-3 \rightarrow$ $+4 \downarrow$

a	$a-3$	$a-6$
$a+4$		$a-2$
$a+8$	$a+5$	$a+2$

(d) $+7 \rightarrow$ $-4 \downarrow$

p	$p+7$	$p+14$	$p+21$
$p-4$			$p+17$
$p-8$			$p+13$
$p-12$	$p-5$	$p+2$	$p+9$

(e) $+3 \rightarrow$ $+4 \downarrow$

b	$b+3$	$b+6$
$b+4$		$b+10$
$b+8$	$b+11$	$b+14$

(f) $-5 \rightarrow$ $+6 \downarrow$

x	$x-5$	$x-10$	$x-15$
$x+6$			$x-9$
$x+12$			$x-3$
$x+18$	$x+13$	$x+8$	$x+3$

2 (a) 64   (b) 62   (c) 52

(d) 59   (e) 64   (f) 53

3 (a) $t+9$ (b) $m+3$ (c) $e+4$

(d) $c+1$ (e) $f-7$ (f) $d-1$

Section C (p 26)

1 A and F $(2h + 8)$ B and E $(2h - 6)$
   D and G $(2h - 9)$

2 A and F $(2x - 10)$ B and C $(2x + 5)$
   E and H $(2x + 12)$

3 (a) $2m + 3$ (b) $2a - 3$ (c) $3y - 9$
   (d) $2d - 7$ (e) $2k + 16$ (f) $3e + 3$
   (g) $2t - 4$ (h) $3n - 7$

11 Pie charts

Pupils interpret a range of simple pie charts. They use 'scaled' charts
and read these to give answers as numbers, fractions and simple
percentages.

p 62	**A** Into parts	Reading pie charts scaled to the number in a survey
p 64	**B** Out of 10	Using pie charts with units of 10%
p 65	**C** Bigger surveys	Using 10% pie charts where there were multiples of 10 participants in a survey

Essential	Optional
Sheets 273 and 274	Coloured crayons
Practice booklet pages 27 and 28	

A **Into parts** (p 62)

Pupils read information from pie charts that are scaled to the number of
units in the survey. Answers are expressed as numbers or as fractions of
the total. Some revision of equivalent fractions may be appropriate.

> Sheet 273
> Optional: Coloured crayons

'They liked this – it was fun.'

◊ When pupils have drawn their pie charts they can be asked questions
such as:

* Do you sleep more at the weekend than in the week?
* What fraction of a weekday do you spend sleeping?

Pupils could make up questions to ask other pupils about the pie charts
that have been drawn.

B **Out of 10** (p 64)

In this section percentages are used where there are only 10 people in a
survey and therefore all readings are in units of 10%.

> Sheet 274
> Optional: Coloured crayons

T

◊ When pupils choose their own topics it is important that they give a reasonable number of options and that someone is likely to choose each one. This is a useful experience in survey design.

ℂ **Bigger surveys** (p 65)

Pupils use the 10% units pie charts to read information where the number in a survey is a multiple of 10.

T

◊ The key point in the housework example is that if there are 50 people then 10% is 5 people.

A spreadsheet makes drawing a pie chart very easy, compared with the computational and graphical effort of drawing one manually. Pupils can draw pie charts from their own data, and conducting a small survey within the class is a motivating way to generate this data.

𝔸 **Into parts** (p 62)

A1 (a) 6   (b) 3
(c) (i) $\frac{18}{36} = \frac{1}{2}$ (ii) $\frac{9}{36} = \frac{1}{4}$

A2 (a) 7   (b) $\frac{6}{24} = \frac{1}{4}$
(c) (i) $\frac{2}{24} = \frac{1}{12}$ (ii) $\frac{5}{24}$

A3 (a) Grey   (b) 4
(c) $\frac{8}{20} = \frac{2}{5}$ (d) $\frac{5}{20} = \frac{1}{4}$

A4 (a) (i) $\frac{1}{4}$ (ii) 9
(b) 3

A5 (a) 40   (b) 25   (c) 16
(d) $\frac{15}{100} = 15\%$

A6 (a) (i) $\frac{1}{10}$ (ii) 10%
(b) $\frac{2}{10} = \frac{1}{5}$ (c) $\frac{3}{10}$
(d) (i) 6   (ii) 18

𝔹 **Out of 10** (p 64)

B1 (a) 4   (b) 10%   (c) 30%   (d) 50%

B2 (a) 50%   (b) 5   (c) 20%   (d) 80%

B3 (a) 35%   (b) 7   (c) 5   (d) 15%

ℂ **Bigger surveys** (p 65)

C1 (a) 30%   (b) 15   (c) 20

C2 (a) (i) 10%   (ii) 3
(b) 9   (c) 12   (d) 6

C3 (a) 15%   (b) 25%   (c) 250   (d) 500

What progress have you made? (p 66)

1 (a) 4   (b) $\frac{5}{20} = \frac{1}{4}$ (c) 50%

Practice booklet

Section A (p 27)

1 (a) 12   (b) 3   (c) $\frac{10}{30} = \frac{1}{3}$
(d) $\frac{5}{30} = \frac{1}{6}$

2 (a) 8   (b) $\frac{8}{25}$ (c) $\frac{5}{25} = \frac{1}{5}$
(d) $\frac{3}{25}$

Sections B and C (p 28)

1 (a) 50%   (b) 5   (c) 20%   (d) 10%

2 (a) 10%   (b) 2   (c) 40%   (d) 4

3 (a) 25%   (b) 10   (c) 10%
(d) 4   (e) 12

⑫ Probability experiments

This unit contains games and practical experiments for which pupils are asked to make estimates of probabilities. They then use these probabilities to work out the expected number of outcomes if the experiment is repeated many times.

Essential
Dice and counters (one per person)
Coin or counter with different sides
Plastic spoons
Multilink cubes

Practice booklet page 29

Ⓐ **The rope bridge** (p 67)

This section allows pupils to see that different outcomes may result from repeating an experiment and that in general larger samples give better estimates of probabilities.

Dice and counters (one per pupil)

'They found it difficult to estimate the probability first, but it was worthwhile.'

◊ Pupils first play the game individually and the results of each experiment can be discussed with the pupils.

To show the results of the whole class, a dot plot is most convenient. This will show clearly that different outcomes may arise from this experiment. By combining the results of a number of experiments, pupils can see that results 'converge' on a better estimate.

A1 to 4 Instead of pupils doing these questions individually, it may be better to consider them as a class activity.

◊ The theoretical probability of reaching home is $\left(\frac{5}{6}\right)^3 = 0.58$ (to 2 d.p.).

B Estimating probabilities (p 69)

This section provides a variety of experiments and games. Individual results can be combined to give a larger sample, leading to a better estimate of probability.

> Dice and counters (one per person)
> Coin or counter with different sides
> Plastic spoons
> Multilink cubes

◊ It is not necessary for all pupils to complete all the games. However, it may be illuminating if pupils try to guess what they think the probabilities will be before doing each experiment.

◊ The theoretical probabilities (to 2 d.p.) for the games are
Home for tea? 0.20
A bit dicey! 0.50
A moving experience 0.47
The odd one out 0.50

A The rope bridge (p 67)

A1 The pupil's estimate of probability based on 20 combined results

A2 (a) 22 (b) $\frac{22}{50}$ (c) $\frac{28}{50}$

A3 (a) $\frac{43}{100}$ (b) $\frac{57}{100}$

(c) The estimate should be 'better' as it is based on a larger sample.

A5 (a) 86 (b) 215 (c) 430

B Experimental probability (p 69)

B1 (a) 27 (b) 12 (c) 21

B2 60

B3 (a) $\frac{27}{60}$ (b) $\frac{12}{60}$ (c) $\frac{21}{60}$

B4 (a) 270 (b) 120 (c) 210

B5 (a) 28 (b) $\frac{28}{50}$ (c) 560

B6 (a) 8 (b) 17

B7 25

B8 $\frac{8}{25}$

B9 About 32

B10 £150

*B11 (a) £112 (b) £38

What progress have you made? (p 72)

1 (a) (i) 12 (ii) $\frac{12}{20}$

(b) About 60

Practice booklet

Section B (p 29)

1 (a) 27 (b) 50 (c) $\frac{27}{50}$

2 (a)

Flavour	Tally	Freq.
Vanilla	ﬀﬀﬀ II	7
Strawberry	ﬀﬀﬀ III	8
Chocolate	ﬀﬀﬀ	5
Total		20

(b) (i) $\frac{7}{20}$ (ii) $\frac{8}{20}$ (iii) $\frac{5}{20}$

(c) Vanilla 70, Strawberry 80, Chocolate 50

3 (a) About 25 (b) About 500

4 (a) $\frac{1}{6}$ (b) About 20

Review 2 (p 73)

1 (a) $\frac{1}{5}$ (b) $\frac{2}{7}$ (c) $\frac{2}{6} = \frac{1}{3}$ (d) $\frac{3}{8}$

2 (a) 66 million (b) 15 tonnes

3 (a)

$\xrightarrow{-3}$

$+2 \Big\downarrow$
18	15	12
20		14
22	19	16

(b)

$\xrightarrow{-1}$

$+4 \Big\downarrow$
5	4	3
9		7
13	12	11

(c)

$\xrightarrow{+3}$

$-2 \Big\downarrow$
8	11	14	17
6			15
4			13
2	5	8	11

4 (a) R   (b) P   (c) Q

5 (a) $\frac{4}{10} = \frac{2}{5}$ (b) 30%
  (c) 20%, 10 people

6 (a) $m + 2$ (b) $2h + 8$ (c) $k - 12$
  (d) $2f + 3$ (e) $2g + 4$ (f) $3e + 2$

7 (a) 1200   (b) 900   (c) 180

8 (a) 50   (b) 28   (c) $\frac{28}{50}$
  (d) $\frac{22}{50}$ (e) About 88

9 (a) £11.96   (b) £5.46   (c) 5 years

Mixed questions 2 (Practice booklet p 30)

1 Spinner A

2 (a) $\frac{8}{18}$ or $\frac{4}{9}$ (b) $\frac{6}{18}$ or $\frac{1}{3}$ (c) $\frac{4}{18}$ or $\frac{2}{9}$

3 (a) £7.50   (b) 15 kg
  (c) 1.8 m   (d) £0.60

4 £50

5 (a)

$\xrightarrow{-3}$

$+2 \Big\downarrow$
r	$r-3$	$r-6$
$r+2$		$r-4$
$r+4$	$r+1$	$r-2$

(b)

$\xrightarrow{+4}$

$-1 \Big\downarrow$
s	$s+4$	$s+8$
$s-1$		$s+7$
$s-2$	$s+2$	$s+6$

(c)

$\xrightarrow{+1}$

$+5 \Big\downarrow$
t	$t+1$	$t+2$
$t+5$		$t+7$
$t+10$	$t+11$	$t+12$

6 (a) $n + 5$ (b) $k + 5$ (c) $m - 7$
  (d) $2a + 7$ (e) $3d + 4$ (f) $4p + 3$

7 (a) 40%   (b) 15   (c) 5

8 24 lengths front crawl, 21 lengths back-
  stroke, 15 lengths breast-stroke

9 (a) (i) 22   (ii) $\frac{22}{50}$
  (b) $\frac{10}{50}$ or $\frac{1}{5}$ (c) 180

⑬ Division

It is not expected that every pupil works through the whole of this unit.
Those who struggle with sections A and B may be confused by section
C and are unlikely to be ready for section D onwards; those who are
ready for sections D, E and F should not not need to complete every
question in the earlier sections.

Practice booklet pages 32 to 36

🅐 The great divide (p 75)

◊ The discussion in the initial activity should bring out different ways to
approach division based on the four ways to think about $60 \div 5$ shown
on the page. These approaches can be referred back to as pupils work
through the unit.

'The pupils made up
their own problems
using the code in A2
and gave them to
others to solve. This
went really well.'

You may wish to teach the traditional 'short division' algorithm where the
calculation is set out as $5\overline{)60}$; some pupils will be quite happy with this
method. Others will prefer a 'chunking' method. For example:

$$
\begin{array}{rr}
\mathbf{10} \times 5 \text{ gives} & 50 \\
\mathbf{2} \times 5 \text{ gives} & + 10 \\
\hline
& 60
\end{array}
$$

$$\mathbf{10} + \mathbf{2} = 12 \text{ so}$$
$$60 \div 5 = 12$$

◊ Pupils can consider a variety of mental methods for simple divisions. They can try to calculate 60 ÷ 5 in their heads and their methods can be discussed and related to written methods where appropriate.

◊ The class could play 'Division bingo'. Pupils make grids and put in some numbers from 1 to 12 (you need to decide if a number can appear more than once). You call out divisions (15 ÷ 5 etc.) and pupils cross off the answer if it appears on their grid.

B Remainders (p 76)

◊ The key issue in this section is whether to round up or down to the nearest whole number. The initial examples can be used to discuss this.

C Different ways (p 77)

◊ This section requires pupils to think about the most appropriate method for different divisions. Weaker pupils may find it helpful to stick to the 'chunking' method for all divisions as it leads on to the method described for 'long division' in section E. Others will be able to be more flexible and choose the most appropriate method each time. For example 135 ÷ 5 is often done by thinking of sharing, but 135 ÷ 15 by grouping. Two possible methods are shown on page 77.

For 135 ÷ 5 the 'short division' algorithm could be appropriate or the 'chunking' method could be used as follows:

		or		
10 × 5 gives	50			135
10 × 5 gives	+ 50	**10** × 5 gives		− 50
	100			85
2 × 5 gives	10	**10** × 5 gives		− 50
2 × 5 gives	10			35
2 × 5 gives	+ 10	**7** × 5 gives		− 35
	130			0
1 more 5 gives	135	**10** + **10** + **7** = 27		
		so 135 ÷ 5 = 27		
10 + **10** + **2** + **2** + **2** + **1** = 27				
so 135 ÷ 5 = 27				

The subtraction method has the advantage that it is easier to see how far you have left to go at each stage but pupils often find subtracting hard.

C1 Emphasise that pupils should show their method each time. They should be as clear as they can but are not expected to produce long wordy explanations.

D Multiples of ten (p 79)

◊ Pupils may need to revise multiplying multiples of ten before starting this section.

◊ Emphasise again that the most appropriate method often depends on the problem you are trying to solve. For example, the most appropriate methods for the three problems on the page ($140 \div 20$, $80 \div 2$ and $420 \div 30$) could all be different.

Point out that people often stick to calculating methods they feel most confident with, but encourage pupils to try unfamiliar methods that could be more efficient.

E Further divisions (p 80)

◊ One way to approach these divisions is to use the traditional 'long division' algorithm. Pupils often get into difficulties with this and may find it easier to think of repeatedly adding (or taking away). The division from the choker problem on page 80 is $378 \div 21$ and could be set out as follows:

		or		
10 × 21 gives	210			378
4 × 21 gives	+ 84	**10** × 21 gives		− 210
	294			168
2 × 21 gives	+ 42	**4** × 21 gives		− 84
	336			84
2 × 21 gives	+ 42	**4** × 21 gives		− 84
	378			0
10 + 4 + 2 + 2 = 18		**10 + 4 + 4** = 18		
so 378 ÷ 21 = 18		so 378 ÷ 21 = 18		

Some pupils will reach the answer more quickly or slowly depending on whether they add smaller or bigger 'chunks' each time. Some may overshoot the target and have to backtrack.

◊ Pupils can estimate the rough size of the answer to the choker problem by noting that $400 \div 20 = 20$; you may wish to encourage pupils to try to estimate their answers first.

F Dividing decimals (p 81)

This section extends division to dividing numbers with one decimal place by single-digit whole numbers.

◊ Pupils will need to be able to recall that for example $7 \times 0.5 = 3.5$. This was introduced in earlier SMP Interact materials; unit 1 'Number bites' question D2 gives further practice in these calculations. The 'chunking' method is used in the initial example. In using this method, or a short division method, you will need to stress the importance of keeping decimal points aligned.

This section is also a good opportunity to encourage estimating a result as a check before carrying out the calculation.

Ⓐ The great divide (p 75)

A1 (a) 9 (b) 8 (c) 9 (d) 6
(e) 9 (f) 9 (g) 8 (h) 7
(i) 11 (j) 7 (k) 14 (l) 13
(m) 13 (n) 14 (o) 15

A2 (a) **1** BADGER **2** MONKEY
3 WALRUS **4** DOLPHIN
5 GIRAFFE **6** GORILLA

(b) The pupil's set of divisions that give answers 6, 12, 9, 11, 20, 15 and 14

A3 (a) $24 \div 8 = $ **3** (b) $12 \div$ **3** $= 4$
(c) **20** $\div 5 = 4$ (d) $32 \div$ **4** $= 8$
(e) $42 \div$ **7** $= 6$ (f) **30** $\div 3 = 10$

A4 (a) 2 (b) 4 (c) 6
(d) 20 (e) 32 (f) 72

A5 (a) 5 (b) 6 (c) 8
(d) 18 (e) 40 (f) 54

A6 (a) $20 \div 4$ gives 5 boxes
(b) $42 \div 6$ gives 7 cases
(c) $64 \div 4$ gives 16 cherries
(d) $96 \div 8$ gives 12 pages
(e) $100 \div 5$ gives 20 postcards
(f) $27 \div 3$ gives £9

Ⓑ Remainders (p 76)

B1 (a) 14 (b) 2

B2 (a) 9 (b) 3

B3 (a) 9 remainder 4 (b) 9 remainder 6
(c) 11 remainder 1 (d) 13 remainder 3
(e) 13 remainder 1 (f) 28 remainder 1
(g) 9 remainder 3 (h) 15 remainder 3
(i) 10 remainder 3 (j) 20 remainder 3

B4 8

B5 12

B6 9

B7 8

B8 13

Ⓒ Different ways (p 77)

C1 (a) 25 (b) 28 (c) 60 (d) 26
(e) 36 (f) 15 (g) 15 (h) 25
(i) 12 (j) 21

C2 33

C3 71

C4 16

C5 18 grams

C6 19

C7 (a) 7 (b) 2

C8 (a) 28 (b) 4

C9 (a) (i) 17 (ii) 6
(b) (i) 18 (ii) 13

Ⓓ Multiples of ten (p 79)

D1 (a) 40 (b) 4 (c) 400 (d) 40
(e) 20 (f) 200 (g) 2 (h) 20

D2 (a) 8 (b) 20 (c) 4 (d) 30

D3 A and E (50)   B and D (5)
C and G (20)   H and I (2)
F is the odd one out (200).

D4 (a) 9   (b) 50   (c) 3   (d) 60
(e) 15   (f) 12   (g) 14   (h) 13

D5 (a) 12   (b) 10

D6 (a) 21   (b) 20

D7 (a) 10   (b) 20   (c) 20   (d) 30
(e) 20   (f) 20   (g) 10   (h) 10

𝔼 **Further divisions** (p 80)

E1 (a) 19   (b) 25   (c) 16   (d) 19

E2 4 pounds

E3 29 pounds

E4 33

E5 3 pounds

E6 13 kg

E7 15 kg

E8 34

E9 (a) 14   (b) 11

E10 (a) 26   (b) 10

E11 22

E12 9

E13 (a) $333 \div 9 = 37$ (b) $777 \div 21 = 37$
$444 \div 12 = 37$ $888 \div 24 = 37$
$555 \div 15 = 37$ $999 \div 27 = 37$
$666 \div 18 = 37$

The results are all 37.

𝔽 **Dividing decimals** (p 81)

F1 (a) 9.7   (b) 21.6   (c) 13.5
(d) 13.6   (e) 16.2   (f) 14.2
(g) 13.3   (h) 16.3

F2 (a) 6.7   (b) 23.1
(c) 35.3   (d) 41.8

F3 16.3 kg

F4 3.4 m

F5 15.4 kg

What progress have you made? (p 82)

1 (a) 9   (b) 12   (c) 8

2 7

3 (a) 3   (b) 30   (c) 4

4 (a) 31   (b) 12   (c) 11
(d) 23 remainder 2   (e) 24
(f) 17 remainder 6   (g) 25
(h) 18 remainder 2

5 (a) 13.4   (b) 16.5   (c) 23.3

Practice booklet

Section A (p 32)

1 (a) 6   (b) 5   (c) 9   (d) 3
(e) 11   (f) 9   (g) 15   (h) 19
(i) 14   (j) 21

2 (a) 5   (b) 15   (c) 11   (d) 18
(e) 9   (f) 81   (g) 7   (h) 72
(i) 5

3 (a) $72 \div 6$ gives 12 boxes
(b) $32 \div 4$ gives 8 sweets
(c) $42 \div 3$ gives 14 pots
(d) $20 \div 5$ gives 4 packs
(e) $88 \div 8$ gives 11 bunches
(f) $56 \div 7$ gives £8

Section B (p 33)

1 (a) 7 remainder 1   (b) 7 remainder 3
(c) 4 remainder 4   (d) 11 remainder 2
(e) 4 remainder 5   (f) 11 remainder 2
(g) 13 remainder 2   (h) 14 remainder 2
(i) 21 remainder 1   (j) 12 remainder 1

2 (a) 7   (b) 5

3 (a) 13   (b) 3

4 (a) 4   (b) 6

5 6

6 9

Section C (p 34)

1 (a) 11   (b) 14   (c) 15   (d) 16
    (e) 13   (f) 16   (g) 36   (h) 25
    (i) 33   (j) 52

2 (a) 37   (b) 2

3 26

4 15 grams

5 (a) 14   (b) 7 cm

6 (a) 17   (b) 15

7 (a) 234   (b) 13

Section D (p 35)

1 (a) 30   (b) 300 (c) 3   (d) 30
    (e) 20   (f) 2   (g) 20   (h) 200

2 (a) 5   (b) 30   (c) 4   (d) 4

3 (a) 5   (b) 50   (c) 60   (d) 6

4 (a) 60   (b) 4   (c) 8   (d) 40
    (e) 8   (f) 11   (g) 7   (h) 17

5 (a) 6   (b) 10

6 (a) 15   (b) 10

Section E (p 35)

1 (a) 18   (b) 19   (c) 17   (d) 21

2 15

3 23

4 12

5 (a) 17   (b) 22

6 (a) 24   (b) 12

7 18

Section F (p 36)

1 (a) 8.3   (b) 8.4   (c) 12.3
    (d) 16.4   (e) 22.3   (f) 26.7
    (g) 36.3   (h) 41.3

2 15.4 kg

⑭ Bottles (p 83)

The information is divided into two sections. The first is intended as a basis for oral questions to be done mentally. The second section is intended for calculator practice and questions could be given in oral or written form. Alternatively pupils could use pencil and paper methods in the second section rather than a calculator.

Start with easy questions to familiarise pupils with the examples. The questions below are exemplars of the types of question you could ask. After giving other questions of your own, you could ask pupils to make up their own, with answers.

Easy starters

1 How many different sizes of Bloom are there? (3)

2 How much is in the largest bottle of perfume? (250 ml)

3 Which bottle of men's cologne costs the least? (Kinetic)

Perfume
One-step calculations

1 How much would a bottle of Amar and a bottle of Exclusif cost altogether? (£45)

2 What is the difference in price of a bottle of Amar and the 50 ml bottle of Bloom? (£5)

3 How many millilitres of perfume would there be in four bottles of Fleur? (120 ml)

4 How much would 5 bottles of Cupid cost? (£125)

5 How many small bottles of Bloom would fit into the largest? (4)

6 How much Cupid perfume do you get for £1? (3 ml)

7 How much does 1 ml of Exclusif cost? (£2)

8 How many bottles of Fleur can you buy for £60? (3)

9 Two sisters are buying their mum a bottle of Cupid. If they share the cost equally, how much do they each pay? (£12.50)

Two-step calculations

1 How much would I pay for two small bottles of Bloom and a bottle of Cupid? (£57)

2 I buy a bottle of Amar and a bottle of Fleur. I get £5 off with a voucher. How much do I pay? (£38)

3 How much would 100 ml of Dada cost? (£250)

4 How much do you save by buying one 100 ml bottle of Bloom, rather than four 25 ml bottles? (£14)

5 How much cheaper is 250 ml of Grosso than 250 ml of Amar? (£75)

6 Which gives you more for your money, Dada or Exclusif? Explain why. (Exclusif, with the pupil's explanation)

Men's cologne

Only one of the exemplar questions below gives a calculator answer that needs rounding. You may wish to include some examples of your own that lead to rounding if pupils have completed unit 3 'Decimals'.

One-step calculations

1 How much would a bottle of Hunk and a bottle of Kinetic cost altogether? (£28.36)

2 What is the difference in price of a bottle of Hunk and the 50 ml bottle of Image? (£5.52)

3 How much change would I get from a £20 note if I bought a bottle of Kinetic? (£10.11)

4 What would be the cost of 3 bottles of Kinetic? (£29.67)

5 How much cologne would 6 bottles of Lance contain? (270 ml)

6 How many bottles of Javelin can you buy for £50? (3)

7 Three friends share the cost of a 100 ml bottle of Image. If they share the cost equally, how much do they each pay? (£14.25)

Two-step calculations

1 How much would three bottles of Hunk and a bottle of Lance cost? (£85.40)

2 How much would 300 ml of Macho cost? (£131.36)

3 How much do you save by buying one 100 ml bottle of Image, rather than four 25 ml bottles? (£7.25)

4 Which gives you more for your money, Kinetic or Javelin? Explain why. (Javelin, with the pupil's explanation)

5 Which is the best value for money, Hunk or Macho? Explain why. (Hunk, with the pupil's explanation)

6 A shop has an offer where if you buy two bottles of cologne, the cheaper one is half price.
What would a bottle of Hunk and a bottle of Javelin cost under this offer?
(£26.77 (26.765))

⑮ Transformations

This unit revises reflections and rotations and introduces the idea of translation. In each section it is important to ensure that pupils understand and can use the vocabulary associated with the relevant transformation.

Essential	**Optional**
Tracing paper, squared paper Sheets 275, 276, 277, 278, 279, 280, 281, 282	OHP transparencies of sheets 275, 277, 279 Small mirrors
Practice booklet pages 37 to 39 (sheet 281 optional)	

𝔸 Reflections (p 84)

This section revises reflecting shapes. The shapes are all drawn on grids. While some pupils will still need tracing paper (or even a mirror) to help them, others will be moving towards using only the grid lines to draw the reflected shape.

The section includes reflections in lines which pass through the shape.

Sheets 275, 276, tracing paper
Optional: OHP transparency of sheet 275, small mirrors

◊ An OHP transparency of sheet 275 could be useful in demonstrating reflections. Pupils who are still unsure could use mirrors on the sheet to visualise where the images are before using tracing paper or just the grid to draw them.

The completed reflections are shown here.

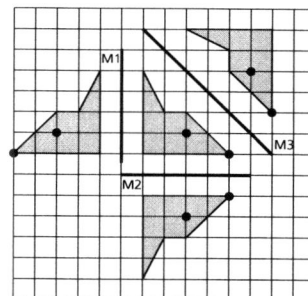

B **Rotations** (p 86)

This section looks at ways of rotating shapes about given points using angles of 180° and 90° clockwise and anticlockwise. Pupils are asked to give descriptions of rotations, incuding the angle and centre of rotation.

Sheets 277, 278, 279, 280, tracing paper
Optional: OHP transparencies of sheets 277, 279

◊ At this stage pupils are only asked to rotate about a point at a corner or on a straight edge of the shape.

◊ In the teacher-led activities pupils should try rotating a shape

• using tracing paper, perhaps with an arrow drawn vertically from the centre of rotation to help see the angle gone through

• using the gridlines to establish where the shape will lie after the rotation

The rotations in the initial activities give:

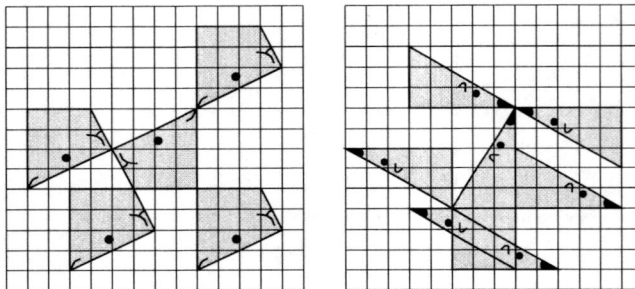

C **Translations** (p 88)

Sheets 281, 282, tracing paper

In your introduction, bring out that every point on the original figure moves exactly the same distance across and up. So to describe a translation, we only need say what happens to one point as it moves.

Each of A, B and C have moved one square to the right and four squares up.
A simple description such as this is all that is required at this stage.

The translations of Millie are shown here.

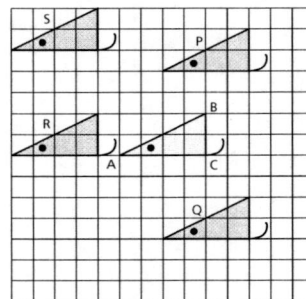

$\mathbb{D}$ **Patterns** (p 89)

Pupils consolidate the language of transformations by describing transformations on simple patterns.

A basic pattern drawn on a piece of acetate may be useful in demonstrating the different transformations.

Practice booklet (p 39)

Optional: sheet 281 (for sections C and D, question 1)

1 Instead of drawing Millie on squared paper, pupils can use the copy of sheet 281 that they used in the introduction to section C, or a fresh copy.

$\mathbb{A}$ **Reflections** (p 84)

A1

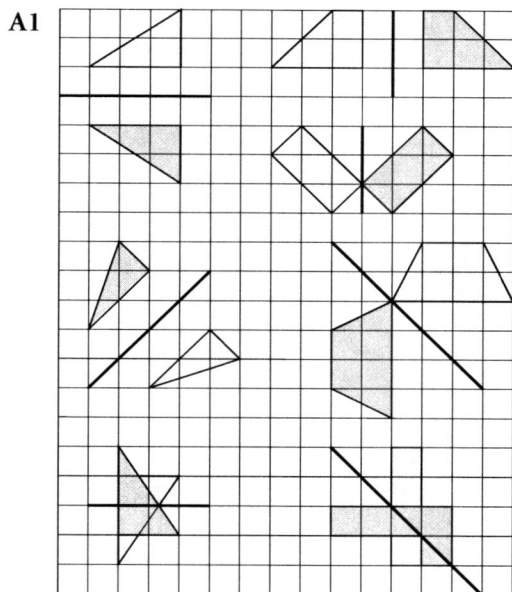

A2 (a) H (b) I (c) G (d) F
A3 (a) M1 (b) M3 (c) M2 (d) M2

$\mathbb{B}$ **Rotations** (p 86)

B1 (a)

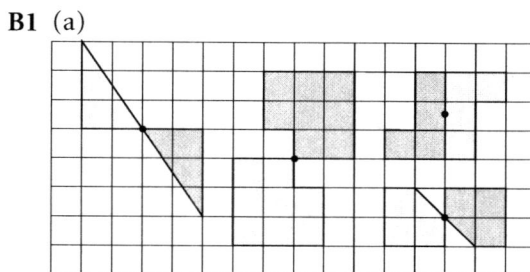

(b)

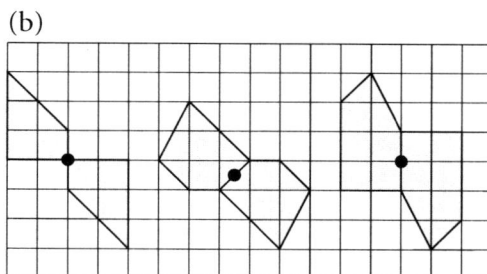

B2 (a)

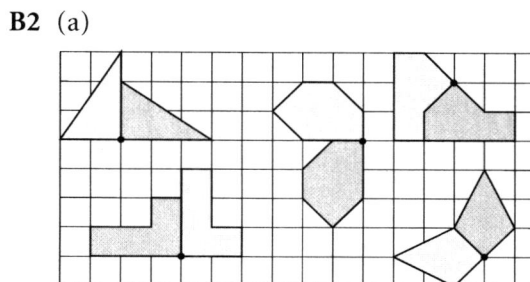

B2 (b)

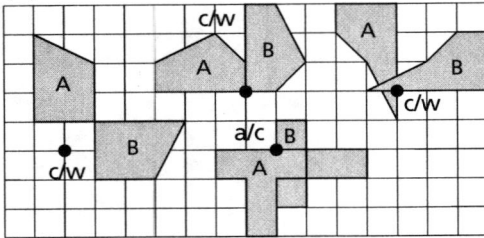

B3 (a) 180° rotation about point C

    (b) 90° anticlockwise rotation about point A

    (c) 90° clockwise rotation about point D

    (d) 180° rotation about point B

B4

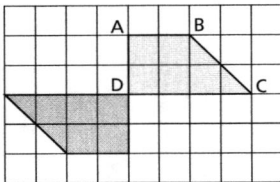

B5 (a)

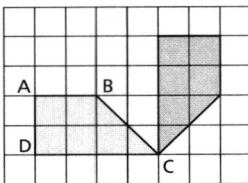

(b) 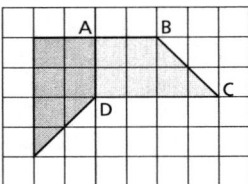   (c)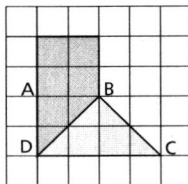

ℂ **Translations** (p 88)

C1 1 right and 4 up

C2 (a) (None across and) 5 down

    (b) 8 right and 1 up

    (c) 7 right (and none up)

    (d) 8 left and 6 down

C3 (a), (b)

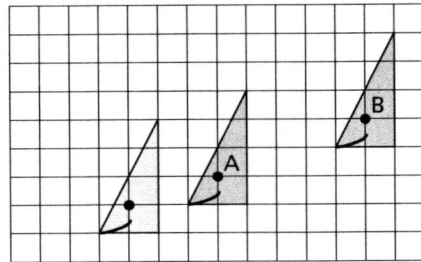

(c) 8 squares to the right and 3 up

𝔻 **Patterns** (p 89)

D1 (a) 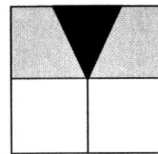   (b)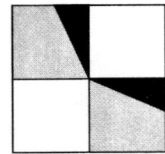

D2 (a) 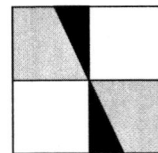   (b)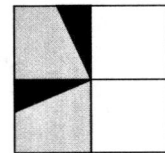

What progress have you made? (p 90)

1–3

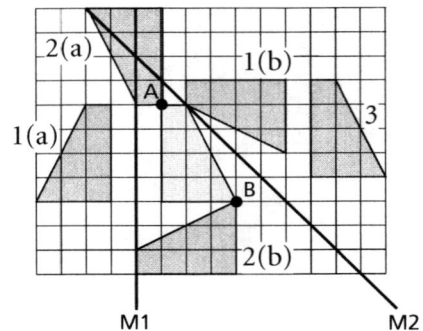

4 (a) 90° anticlockwise rotation about the centre

    (b) Reflection in line M2

    (c) Reflection in line M3

Practice booklet

Section A (p 37)

1

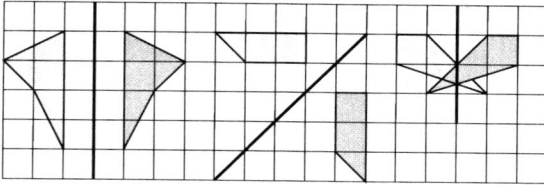

2 (a) M2 (b) M1 (c) M3 (d) M3

3 (a) C (b) B (c) G (d) F

Section B (p 38)

1

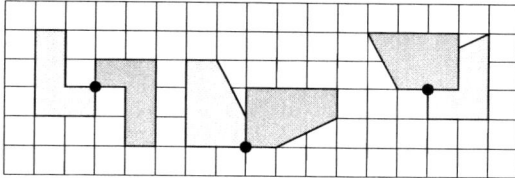

2 (a) Centre C, 90° anticlockwise
  (b) Centre C, 180°
  (c) Centre C, 90° clockwise
  (d) Centre A, 90° clockwise

Sections C and D (p 39)

1

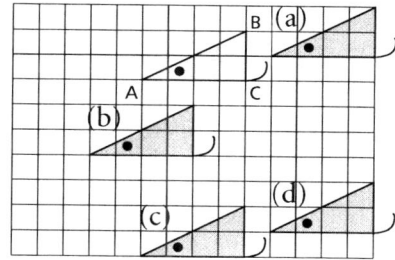

2 (a) 3 squares left and 3 up
  (b) 5 squares right
  (c) 3 squares right and 1 down
  (d) 4 squares left and 2 down
  (e) 6 squares right and 5 up

3

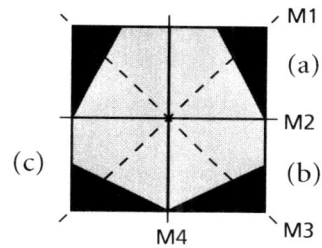

4 The pupil's design and descriptions

⑯ Groundwork (p 91)

This unit gives an opportunity for pupils to practise finding the areas and perimeters of rectangles and composite shapes in context. The work on composite shapes extends to cases where a rectangle is removed and leads into finding the areas of simple right-angled triangles.

1 (a) $15\,cm^2$, $16\,cm$
  (b) $54\,cm^2$, $30\,cm$
  (c) $84\,cm^2$, $38\,cm$
  (d) $200\,cm^2$, $66\,cm$

2 (a) $40\,m^2$ (b) $180\,m^2$
  (c) $64\,m^2$ (d) $2500\,m^2$

3 (a) $26\,m$ (b) $54\,m$
  (c) $32\,m$ (d) $250\,m$

4 (a) $12\,m^2$ (b) $15\,m^2$
  (c) $27\,m^2$ (d) £270

5 (a) The pupil's sketch with missing lengths added
  (b) The floor split into two rectangles
  (c) The areas of the pupil's rectangles
  (d) $60\,m^2$

6 (a) $28\,m^2$ (b) $40\,m^2$ (c) $66\,m^2$

7 (a) $x = 3\,m$, $y = 4\,m$
  (b) $30\,m$ (c) 8 rolls

8 (a) $70\,m^2$ (b) $8\,m^2$ (c) $62\,m^2$

9 (a) $60\,m^2 - 24\,m^2 = 36\,m^2$
  (b) $150\,m^2 - 15\,m^2 = 135\,m^2$

10 $21\,m^2 - 12\,m^2 = 9\,m^2$

11 (a) $\frac{1}{2}$ (b) $12\,cm^2$ (c) $6\,cm^2$

12 A $10\,cm^2$ B $5\,cm^2$
   C $7.5\,cm^2$ D $8\,cm^2$

Practice booklet (p 40)

1 (a) $18\,cm^2$, $18\,cm$
  (b) $56\,cm^2$, $30\,cm$
  (c) $70\,m^2$, $34\,m$
  (d) $300\,m^2$, $70\,m$

2 (a) $26\,m^2$ (b) $60\,m^2$

3 (a) $750\,m^2$ (b) $80\,m^2$
  (c) $670\,m^2$ (d) $36\,m$

⑰ Number relationships

This unit provides revision on multiples, factors and square numbers. It includes several investigations and puzzles. Square roots are introduced as the inverse of squares.

Number bites W1 and W4 to W6 on pages 4 and 5 offer suitable revision for weaker pupils before they start this unit.

p 94	**A** Multiples
p 95	**B** Factors
p 96	**C** Prime numbers
p 97	**D** Squares and square roots

Essential	Optional
Squared paper	Coloured pens or pencils
Practice booklet pages 41 and 42	

Ⓐ **Multiples** (p 94)

> Squared paper
> Optional: Coloured pens or pencils

A2 Pupils could also look at other ways of deciding whether a large number is a multiple of another number, such as:

A number is a multiple of …
- 6 if it is a multiple of 3 and even
- 4 if the last two digits are divisible by 4
- 8 if half of it is divisible by 4
- 9 if the sum of its digits is divisible by 9

A5 Pupils could make up their own puzzles like these. If they give them to others to do they will probably discover that there are not always unique answers. This can be discussed.

Patchwork patterns

◊ This activity is designed to allow practice in finding multiples rather than to form the basis of an in-depth investigation. More able pupils might consider how the pattern is affected by the way the spiral is formed.

B Factors (p 95)

In finding all the factors of a number pupils should be encouraged to use a systematic approach using multiplication pairs. They should list the factors in numerical order.

B4 You may wish to draw attention to the fact that the sentence remaining (Was it a cat I saw?) is palindromic.

Multiples and factors bingo

You will need to call out statements such as 'A multiple of 7' or 'A factor of 36'.

Pupils could be asked to choose their own numbers between 1 and 40 and after playing discuss what numbers were good ones to pick.

C Prime numbers (p 96)

Squared paper

The sieve of Eratosthenes

◊ The prime numbers will not fall through the sieve – encourage pupils to describe these numbers as clearly as they can in their own words. The primes that it reveals will depend on the number of squares on the width of the paper.
Eratosthenes of Cyrene (276–194 BC) was a Greek poet, astronomer, mathematician, historian and athlete. He was librarian of the University of Alexandria. Apart from the 'sieve', he is well known for measuring the circumference of the Earth by observing the direction of the Sun at two places a great distance apart.

D Squares and square roots (p 97)

Happy numbers

◊ This can be organised very successfully as a class activity, with different pupils investigating different numbers. The results can then be combined in one big diagram. A chart can be produced showing how many stages it takes for each starting number.

The happy numbers between 0 and 50 are
          1, 7, 10, 13, 19, 23, 28, 31, 32, 44, 49

Ⓐ Multiples (p 94)

A1 (a) 4, 8, 12, 16, 20, 24, 28, 52
 (b) 6, 9, 12, 15, 18, 21, 24, 27, 30
 (c) 5, 10, 15, 20, 25, 30
 (d) 6, 11, 16, 21, 26, 71
 (e) 5, 8, 11, 14, 17, 20, 23, 26, 29, 53, 71

A2 165, 237, 2652, 7632, 26 571

A3 Any multiple of 60

A4 171

A5 (a) **2**7 (b) **5**4 (c) **8**1
 (d) **3**6 (e) 15**3** (f) **2**0**7**
 (g) **5**0**4** (h) **9**00 (i) 1**8**00

Ⓑ Factors (p 95)

B1 1, 2, 4, 5, 10, 20

B2 (a) $1 \times 21 = 21$, $3 \times 7 = 21$,
  so factors are 1, 3, 7 and 21
 (b) $1 \times 18 = 18$, $2 \times 9 = 18$, $3 \times 6 = 18$,
  so factors are 1, 2, 3, 6, 9 and 18
 (c) $1 \times 48 = 48$, $2 \times 24 = 48$, $3 \times 16 = 48$,
  $4 \times 12 = 48$, $6 \times 8 = 48$,
  so factors are 1, 2, 3, 4, 6, 8, 12, 16, 24, 48
 (d) $1 \times 30 = 30$, $2 \times 15 = 30$, $3 \times 10 = 30$,
  $5 \times 6 = 30$,
  so factors are 1, 2, 3, 5, 6, 10, 15, 30
 (e) $1 \times 16 = 16$, $2 \times 8 = 16$, $4 \times 4 = 16$,
  so factors are 1, 2, 4, 8, 16

B3 (a) 20 — 4, 10, 20, 2, 5, 1
 (b) 18 — 3, 9, 18, 2, 6, 1
 (c) 36 — 6, 36, 18, 4, 12, 3, 9, 2, 6, 1
 (d) 42 — 6, 42, 21, 3, 14, 2, 7, 1
 (e) 23 — 23 — 1

B4 Was it a cat I saw?

Ⓒ Prime numbers (p 96)

C1 37 and 19 are prime.
 27, 51 and 33 are not.

C2 Only 83 is prime.

Ⓓ Squares and square roots (p 97)

D1 36, 49 and 100

D2 Do not hide in a tree.

D3 $1^2 + 4^2 + 6^2 + 7^2 = 2^2 + 3^2 + 5^2 + 8^2$

D4 (a) 3 (b) 8 (c) 5 (d) 7

D5 (a) 6 (b) 2 (c) 9 (d) 10

D6 (a) 8 (b) 1 (c) 3 (d) 7

D7 (a) 14 (b) 25 (c) 19
 (d) 23 (e) 29 (f) 27.36…
 (g) 14.21… (h) 16.24…

What progress have you made? (p 98)

1 The pupil's four multiples of 6

2 40, 72, 56

3 (a) 1, 2, 3, 4, 6, 8, 12, 16, 24, 48
 (b) 1, 2, 3, 5, 6, 10, 15, 30
 (c) 1, 2, 3, 4, 6, 9, 12, 18, 36
 (d) 1, 2, 4, 5, 10, 20, 25, 50, 100

4 64, 36 and 25

5 (a) 9 (b) 20 (c) 11 (d) 18.57…

Practice booklet

Sections A and B (p 41)

1 (a) 20, 30 (b) 20, 25, 30, 35
 (c) 12, 16, 20, 36 (d) 12, 36

2 (a) 23**1** or 234 or 237
 (b) 232 or 236
 (c) 234

3 (a) No   (b) Teddy

   (c) No   (d) Lollipop

   (e) Teddy

   (f) Teddy and lollipop

4 (a) $1 \times 15, 3 \times 5$

     so factors of 15 are 1, 3, 5, 15

   (b) $1 \times 27, 3 \times 9$

     so factors of 27 are 1, 3, 9, 27

   (c) $1 \times 32, 2 \times 16, 4 \times 8$

     so factors of 32 are 1, 2, 4, 8, 16, 32

   (d) $1 \times 36, 2 \times 18, 3 \times 12, 4 \times 9, 6 \times 6$

     so factors of 36 are 1, 2, 3, 4, 6, 9, 12, 18, 36

5 (a) 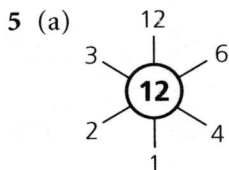   (b)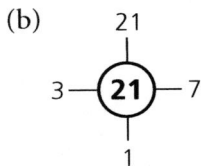

   (c) 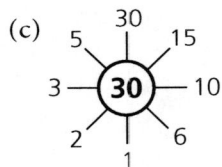   (d)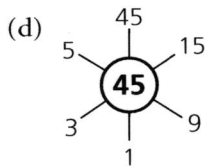

6 5

Sections C and D (p 42)

1 11, 13, 17, 19, 23, 29

2 97, 109, 137

3 (a) 1   (b) 25   (c) 81   (d) 121

4 Yes, 8 slabs by 8 slabs

5 (a) 2   (b) 4   (c) 6   (d) 7

6 (a) 7   (b) 9

7 (a) 13   (b) 17   (c) 22   (d) 31

18 Simplifying

p 99	**A** Perimeters	Simplifying expressions such as $3n + 4 + 2n - 3$
p 101	**B** Missing lengths	Simplifying expressions such as $3n + 4 - 2n - 3$
p 103	**C** Hollow magic squares	Consolidating work on simplifying expressions Using algebra to show that a simple statement is true

---

Practice booklet pages 43 to 45

🄐 **Perimeters** (p 99)

◊ You could begin the discussion by asking pupils to make sketches of each shape when $n = 2$ for example, and then ask them to work out the perimeters of each shape. The results could be tabulated for different values of n and pupils asked to comment on the results.

Some possible comments are:
- the perimeter of the yellow shape is always double the perimeter of the blue shape
- the perimeter of the green shape is always double the perimeter of the yellow shape
- the perimeters of the green and orange shapes are equal when $n = 1$
- the perimeters of the green and pink shapes are equal when $n = 6$
- the perimeters of the pink and purple shapes are equal for all values of n

◊ Establish that you can find an expression for the perimeter of each shape by adding the expressions for the lengths of each side. Show how to simplify each expression.

Some pupils may find it helpful to see each length divided into smaller parts. For example, the orange shape can be redrawn as follows:

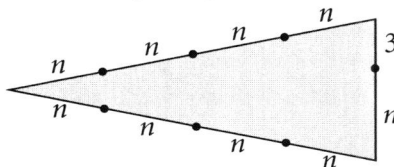

Numerical examples can be used to demonstrate that, for example, 3 times a number added to 4 times a number is equivalent to 7 times that number, e.g. $(3 \times 100) + (4 \times 100) = 7 \times 100$.

Remind pupils that $3n + 4n$ and $7n$ are called equivalent expressions as they have the same value for all values of n.

Once the simplest expressions for the perimeters have been established, pupils can compare them and notice for example that, since the perimeters of the pink and purple shapes are both $10n + 12$, they will always be the same.

◊ Make sure pupils understand that, for example, $9n + 3$ cannot be simplified further. (In some trial schools, it was common for pupils to 'simplify', for example, $8m + m + 5 + 3$ to $17m$.)

Numerical substitution can be used to identify mistakes. For example $9n + 3 \neq 12n$ because when $x = 2$, $9n + 3 = 21$ but $12n = 24$.

A1 In part (b), encourage pupils to use the equivalent expressions they found in part (a) to save themselves work. For example, since B is equivalent to G both must have the same value for $p = 2$.

*A5 This introduces examples with two variables for the first time.

B Missing lengths (p 101)

◊ Pupils could work in pairs trying to sketch each diagram with all the lengths marked in. Use the results to establish that
- $8m - 5m = 3m$
- $6x - 2x = 4x$
- $5x - x = 4x$
- $5m + 2 - 3m = 2m + 2$
- $6m - 3 - 4m = 2m - 3$

◊ Again, numerical substitution can be used to identify mistakes. For example $9n - 3 \neq 6n$ because when $x = 2$, $9n - 3 = 15$ but $6n = 12$.

Missing piece

Pupils should realise that whatever size piece is cut from the 8 cm square the perimeter of the shape will always be 32 cm. This can be shown by Perimeter $= 8 + 8 - y + x + y + 8 - x + 8 = 32$.
This is a useful introduction to the work in section C.

C Hollow magic squares (p 103)

The context for this section is hollow magic squares, where only two rows and two columns need to be made to sum to the same total. Pupils are given the opportunity to use algebra to show that a grid of expressions will *always* form a hollow magic square of numbers.

A Perimeters (p 99)

A1 (a) A and F ($11p$), B and G ($4p + 7$),
C and J ($10p$), D and L ($8p + 2$),
E and K ($3p$), H and I ($5p$)

    (b) A and F: 22   B and G: 15
C and J: 20   D and L: 18
E and K: 6   H and I: 10

A2 (a) $4m$; 12   (b) $7m$; 21
    (c) $2m + 10$; 16   (d) $8m + 2$; 26
    (e) $14m + 2$; 44

A3 (a) $4n$ (b) $7m$ (c) $6k$
    (d) $9m + 8$ (e) $12h$ (f) $7g + 7$
    (g) $8j + 11$ (h) $6e + 2$ (i) $10d - 3$
    (j) $7c + 1$ (k) $5b - 1$ (l) $9a - 4$

A4 (a) $13p$ (b) $2m$
    (c) $n + 5$ (d) $2k + 3$

*A5 (a) $3k$ (b) $3p + 2t$
    (c) $2a + 2b$ (d) $2m + 5$
    (e) $6c + d + 6$ (f) $2x + 8y + 11$

*A6 (a) $2x + 3y$ (b) $5m + n$
    (c) $8p + 5q$ (d) $8g + 8h$
    (e) $j + 9k + 10$ (f) $7x + 5y + 5$
    (g) $2m + 11n$ (h) $5p + 8q + 5$
    (i) $7g + 10h + 9$ (j) $8j + 8k - 10$
    (k) $5a + 7b - 2$ (l) $10c + 5d - 3$

B Missing lengths (p 101)

B1 A and F ($3m$),   B and G ($2m + 6$),
C and E ($4m$),   D and H ($2m - 1$)

B2 (a) $6p$ (b) $4m$ (c) $2k$
    (d) $6h + 5$ (e) $8h$ (f) $3g + 7$
    (g) $2j + 11$ (h) $4e + 2$ (i) $2d - 3$

*B3 (a) $4m + 5$
    (b) (i) $2x + 3$ (ii) $2x - 1$

*B4 (a) $3n$ (b) $9m$ (c) 3

C Hollow magic squares (p 103)

C1 (a)

9	1	8
5		7
4	11	3

(b)

3	2	7
5		4
4	7	1

(c)

1	8	13	12
14			7
4			9
15	10	3	6

C2 (a) Yes   (b) No   (c) No
    (d) Yes   (e) Yes

C3 (a)

7	8	3
2		10
9	4	5

    (b) Yes
    (c) $m + 6 + m + 7 + m + 2 = 3m + 15$
    (d) $3m + 15$
    (e) Each set of three expressions adds to give $3m + 15$.
    (f) Each total is the same so any value of m will give a magic square.
    (g) The pupil's values and magic squares

C4 (a) A and C
    (b) A

7	12	5
6		10
11	4	9

or B

7	14	3
4		12
13	2	9

*C5 B is a hollow magic square.
Rows and columns add to $18p + 3t$.

What progress have you made? (p 105)

1 (a) $3d$ (b) $7c$ (c) $11k$

  (d) $8h + 5$ (e) $11m + 2$ (f) $4n$

  (g) $3b + 4$ (h) $4a + 3$

2 (a) $7x + 10$ (b) $11m + 3$

3 It is not a hollow magic square.
The bottom row adds to $6b + 8$;
the rest add to $6b + 10$.

*4 (a) $3x + 2y$ (b) $9m + 8n$

  (c) $7p + 11q + 7$

Practice booklet

Section A (p 43)

1 (a) Triangle $6n$, rhombus $4n$,
parallelogram $6n$, trapezium $5n$

  (b) Triangle and parallelogram

2 (a) A and E ($7n$), B and F ($5n$),
C and I ($6n$), D and G ($8n + 7$)
H and L ($5n + 7$), J and K ($6n + 5$)

  (b) A and E: 14
B and F: 10
C and I: 12
D and G: 23
H and L: 17
J and K: 17

3 (a) $5w$ (b) $9s$ (c) $13k + 1$

  (d) $5f + 3$ (e) $4j + 2$ (f) $9v + 3$

  (g) $11p + 1$ (h) $8r + 1$ (i) $7m + 11$

4 (a) $6r$ (b) $2w + 4$

*5 (a) $3c + 2d$ (b) $6a + 2b + 10$

  (c) $8a + 8c$ (d) $10m + 6n + 8$

  (e) $5r + 11s + 6$

Section B (p 44)

1 (a) $4m$ (b) $4m$, $m+2$

2 (a) A and E ($4w$), B and F ($7w$),
C and D ($6w + 7$), G and H ($9w + 2$)

  (b) A and E: 12
B and F: 21
C and D: 25
G and H: 29

3 (a) $9p$ (b) $6p$ (c) $7p + 1$

  (d) $7p + 9$ (e) $7p + 3$ (f) $9p$

  (g) $6p$ (h) $7p + 6$

4 (a) $x + 4$ (b) $x + 4$

  (c) $2x$ (d) $2x - 2$

5 (a) $3m$ (b) $5r$ (c) $2d$

  (d) 6 (e) $6p$ (f) $2k$

Section C (p 45)

1 (a)

6	8	3	12
7			5
9			8
7	12	6	4

  (b) Yes   (c) $4m + 21$

  (d) $4m + 21$ (e) $4m + 21$

  (f) The totals are always the same.

  (g) The pupil's magic square

2 B and C

⑲ Two-way tables

This unit invites pupils to record information in two-way tables. By calculating row and column totals they also read information from two-way tables and make statements about simple hypotheses.

p 106 **A** Making tables	Recording data in simple two-way tables
p 108 **B** Reading tables	Reading information from two-way tables
p 109 **C** Experiments	Using two-way tables to analyse simple experiments

Essential	**Optional**
Sheets 283 and 284	Scissors
Practice booklet pages 46 and 47	

Ⓐ **Making tables** (p 106)

Pupils are invited to summarise data, either observed or recorded, in two-way tables.

> Sheets 283 and 284
> Optional: scissors

Toadstools

'Pupils worked in pairs and used colour on the sheet to sort the toadstools.'

It may be easier for some pupils to sort the toadstools by cutting them out and physically sorting them into groups. Other pupils may prefer to sort by crossing off toadstools on the sheet.

After the pupils have completed sorting the toadstools, discuss their results with them and draw up a two-way table summarising the data.

	Spotty	Plain	Total
Collar	5	10	15
No collar	11	4	15
Total	16	14	30

Egg gradings

Dividers or a piece of card 4 cm long are useful in checking the lengths.
Pupils will need showing how to use tallying to record the data.
A two-way table can then be made with totals and discussed.

	Small	Large	Total
Plain	4	8	12
Speckled	4	4	8
Total	8	12	20

B Reading tables (p 108)

Pupils are asked to interpret data recorded in two-way tables.

◊ The widow's peak data is intended to stimulate questions. Some typical questions might be:

• How many boys were in this class?

• How many pupils were in the class altogether?

• Did more pupils have straight hairlines or widow's peaks?

• What fraction of boys had straight hairlines?
  Was this more or less than half of them?

• Who is more likely to have a straight hairline, a boy chosen from this class or a girl? Explain why.

Data could be recorded for the class, but it may not then be easy to compare the likelihood of boys and girls having widow's peaks.

C Experiments (p 109)

This section gives pupils the opportunity to use two-way tables as a means of analysing data from an experiment.

Tongue rolling and attached earlobes are inherited characteristics, as are widow's peaks. Some large-scale research on these characteristics has been carried out on pupils in the USA and data can be found on the internet.

Pupils will need to devise their own recording methods if carrying out their own surveys.

'An interesting experiment – best to do it as a whole class.'

Ⓐ Making tables (p 106)

A1 (a) 30   (b) 14
    (c) $\frac{15}{30} = \frac{1}{2}$ (d) $\frac{5}{16}$

A2 (a) (i) 12   (ii) 8
    (b) $\frac{8}{12} = \frac{2}{3}$ (c) $\frac{4}{8} = \frac{1}{2}$
    (c) The plain eggs

A3 (a) 2   (b) 6   (c) 4   (d) 0

	Girls	Boys	Total
Candlestick	2	6	8
Face	4	0	4
Total	6	6	12

A4 (a) The pupil's tally chart
    (b)

	Boys	Girls	Total
160 cm or less	4	2	6
Taller than 160 cm	3	6	9
Total	7	8	15

    (c) $\frac{3}{7}$ (d) $\frac{6}{8} = \frac{3}{4}$

Ⓑ Reading tables (p 108)

B1 (a) 30   (b) 24
    (c) 38   (d) $\frac{20}{30} = \frac{2}{3}$

*B2 Females (3 times as many could smell than couldn't; only twice the number of males could)

B3 (a) 34   (b) 30   (c) 32   (d) 50%
    (e) Geraniums; although similar amounts of each plant were grown sweet-peas produced only half the number of white flowers that geraniums did.

B4 (a)

	Boys	Girls	Total
Brown eyes	9	12	21
Blue eyes	3	3	6
Total	12	15	27

    (b) 6   (b) $\frac{6}{27} = \frac{2}{9}$

B5 (a) (i) 24   (ii) 18
    (b) $\frac{14}{24} = \frac{7}{12}$
    (c) $\frac{6}{18} = \frac{1}{3}$
    (d) Women (Over half the women were over 80, but less than half the men were.)

Ⓒ Experiments (p 109)

C1 (a)

	Boys	Girls	Total
Attached	6	6	12
Unattached	9	6	15
Total	15	12	27

    (b) 12   (c) 6   (d) $\frac{6}{12} = \frac{1}{2}$
    (e) Girls (Half the girls had attached earlobes, but less than half the boys had.)

What progress have you made? (p 110)

1

	Boys	Girls
Want a uniform	5	10
Don't want a uniform	10	6

2 (a) 15   (b) 40
    (c) $\frac{3}{15} = \frac{1}{5}$ (d) $\frac{20}{25} = \frac{4}{5}$

Practice booklet

Section A (p 46)

1 (a) The pupil's tally chart
    (b)

	Square	Round	Total
Black	2	8	10
White	6	4	10
Total	8	12	20

    (c) 20   (d) 2   (e) 4
    (f) $\frac{10}{20} = \frac{1}{2}$ (g) $\frac{2}{10} = \frac{1}{5}$

2 (a) (i) 1   (ii) 5   (iii) 4   (iv) 8

(b)

	Multiple of 3	Not a multiple of 3	Total
Odd	1	5	6
Even	4	8	12
Total	5	13	18

(c) $\frac{4}{12} = \frac{1}{3}$ (d) $\frac{6}{18} = \frac{1}{3}$

Sections B and C (p 47)

1 (a) 16 (b) 14 (c) 30 (d) 5
(e) 11 (f) $\frac{8}{16} = \frac{1}{2}$

2 (a) 10 (b) 5 (c) 30 (d) 20
(e)

	Boys	Girls	Total
Could identify	5	8	13
Could not identify	5	12	17
Total	10	20	30

(f) 8 (g) 50%

(h) Boys were better at identifying the cola.
Half the boys identified the cola correctly; less than half the girls identified it correctly.

Review 3 (p 111)

1 (a) 6   (b) 9   (c) 13   (d) 17
   (e) 11 remainder 2
   (f) 7 remainder 4
   (g) 8 remainder 6
   (h) 13 remainder 1
   (i) 32   (j) 22   (k) 8   (l) 7
   (m) 40   (n) 9   (o) 14   (p) 23

2 (a) 90° clockwise rotation about point B
   (b)

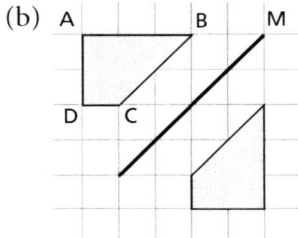

3 (a)

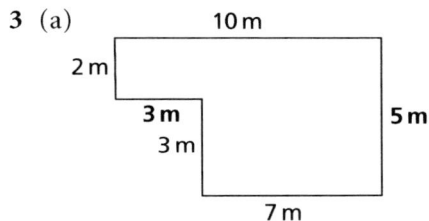

   (b) 41 m^2

4 (a) 30 m   (b) 6 rolls

5 THIS IS EASY

6 (a) 24   (b) 16

7 (a) $p + p + 4 = 2p + 4$
   (b) $3f + 3k + f + 2k = 4f + 5k$
   (c) $3m + 3m + 3 + 2s + 3 = 6m + 2s + 6$

8 (a) 20   (b) $\frac{15}{20} = \frac{3}{4}$
   (c) 50   (d) 54%

9 (a) $3p + 1$ (b) $3p + 2$ (c) $3p + 1$
   (d) $2p + 3$ (e) $3p + 3$ (f) $3p$
   (a) and (c) are the same length.

10 (a) £4.72   (b) £5   (c) £1.53

Mixed questions 3 (Practice booklet p 48)

1 (a) 14 bags   (b) 10

2 (a) 5.3   (b) 40.8   (c) 47.7

3

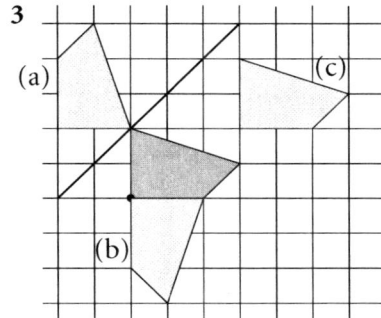

4 (a) One possible way is shown here.

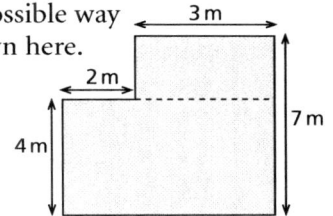

   (b) 9 m^2 and 20 m^2 or 8 m^2 and 21 m^2
   (c) 29 m^2 (d) 24 m

5 (a) 32   (b) 2   (c) 2   (d) 25

6 (a) 16   (b) 21   (c) 24   (d) 31

7 (a) $2k$ (b) t (c) 4

8 (a) $4n$ (b) $5p$ (c) $7d + 2$
   (d) $4s$ (e) $a + 1$ (f) $2q + 6$

9 (a)

	Boys	Girls	Total
Swim	8	6	14
Not swim	6	6	12
Total	14	12	26

   (b) 12   (c) $\frac{8}{14}$ or $\frac{4}{7}$ (d) $\frac{6}{12}$ or $\frac{1}{2}$

10 £159.30

11 (a) £318.23   (b) £9.09

⑳ Angles and lines

This unit invites pupils to explore angle properties such as angles on a line, angles round a point and angles in a triangle. The unit also provides some practice in drawing triangles.

Although the unit is based on pencil and paper investigations it is recommended that use be made of software packages.

T	p 113 **A** Angles on lines	Revision of estimating and measuring angles; angles on a straight line
T	p 116 **B** Angles round a point	
T	p 118 **C** Triangles	Using the fact that angles in a triangle add up to 180°
T	p 119 **D** Drawing triangles	Drawing triangles in the SSS, SAS and ASA cases
	p 121 **E** 3-D shapes	Drawing simple nets

Essential	**Optional**
Angle measurers, compasses	Dynamic geometry package
Sheet 285 printed on card	Commercial sets of polygons
Plain paper and scissors	Tracing paper or acetate sheets

Practice booklet pages 50 to 53 (needs compasses, angle measurer, scissors)

🅐 Angles on lines (p 113)

The aim of this section is for pupils to use the fact that angles on a straight line add up to 180°.

> Angle measurers
> Optional: computers or graphical calculators with dynamic geometry, tracing paper or acetate sheets

Introductory activities

Are you being obtuse?

This can be used as a simple reminder of the definitions of the terms acute, obtuse and reflex. Pupils may either draw the angles on paper or use two sheets of tracing paper or acetate with a line drawn on each one.

Estimating angles

This could be played as a game between two pupils. Each pupil chooses an angle from the list (or one of their own) and the other tries to draw it. Points could be awarded if they are within given limits.

A dynamic geometry package can be used in this section for estimating angles – two line segments could be placed to estimate a given angle. The angle can then be measured and checked.

Angles on a straight line

Pupils should try several different positions of one line touching the other and measuring the angles. Inevitably the sum will not always come to 180° due to inaccuracies in measurement.

A dynamic geometry package can be used by drawing the lines on screen and showing the value of each angle. By moving the end of the second line it can be seen that whatever the value of the two angles, they always add up to 180°.

Ⓑ Angles round a point (p 116)

The main objective of this section is for pupils to discover and use the fact that angles around a point must add up to 360°.

> Angle measurers
> Sheet 285 (preferably on card)
> Optional: commercial sets of polygons

Fitting round a point (p 116)

Once pupils have measured the internal angles of the shapes on the sheet they can look at which combinations of shapes fit around a point. By adding together the angles they should discover that they always add to 360°. Other shapes could be introduced but the ones here give a wide range of options. The significance of this work in designing tessellations could also be explored.

◊ As with angles on a line, dynamic geometry could be used where three or more lines are made to meet at a point and the values of the angles formed are shown. By moving the free ends of the lines the fact that the sum of the angles is always 360° can be shown.

Star patterns (p 117)

This gives an excellent opportunity for pupils to use Logo.

C **Triangles** (p 118)

Pupils use the fact that the sum of the three angles in any triangle is 180°.

> Optional: plain paper, scissors

◊ In the introductory activity pupils could cut out their own triangles drawn on card and compare their results with others. Alternatively the result could be demonstrated easily by laying the pieces on an OHP. Pupils could be encouraged to try to draw a triangle where this doesn't work.

◊ A triangle could be drawn using a dynamic geometry package with the values of the angles at the vertices showing. By moving the vertices it can be seen that the angles always add to 180°.

D **Drawing triangles** (p 119)

In this section pupils are asked to draw triangles given either SAS or ASA information. Some may still lack the manipulative skills needed to use ruler and compasses and the patterns and other tasks provide practice in these.

> Compasses, angle measurers, plain paper

Triangle puzzle

This puzzle allows pupils to practise drawing triangles given different information.

The solution to the puzzle is

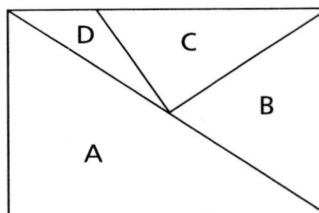

E **3-D shapes** (p 121)

Pupils should have met nets of cuboids earlier. Here they meet nets of other 3-D shapes, and use some of the drawing skills practised in the unit.

> Compasses, angle measurer, scissors

A Angles on lines (p 113)

A1 (a) 101° (obtuse) (b) 262° (reflex)
(c) 220° (reflex) (d) 18° (acute)
(e) 62° (acute) (f) 299° (reflex)
(g) 139° (obtuse)

A2 (a) A: 125° B: 150°
C: 70° D: 30°
E: 110° F: 55°
(b) A and F; B and D; C and E

A3 (a) No
(b) acute + obtuse and
right angle + right angle

A4 $a = 115°$ $b = 50°$ $c = 160°$
$d = 133°$ $e = 120°$ $f = 30°$
$g = 65°$ $h = 72°$ $i = 50°$

A5 The pupil's copy of the pattern

B Angles round a point (p 116)

B1 Q has been cut from A.
S has been cut from B.
P has been cut from C.
R has been cut from D.

B2 $a = 70°$ $b = 250°$ $c = 90°$ $d = 230°$
$e = 80°$ $f = 110°$ $g = 60°$ $h = 160°$

B3 (a) 120°
(b) An equilateral triangle

B4 90°

B5 (a) 72°
(b) The pupil's drawing of an inscribed regular pentagon

B6 (a) The pupil's drawing of an inscribed regular hexagon
(b) The pupil's drawing of an inscribed regular octagon

B7 (a) 30° (b) 18°

C Triangles (p 118)

C1 $a = 60°$ $b = 40°$ $c = 35°$ $d = 88°$

C2 $a = 50°$ $b = 15°$ $c = 60°$ $d = 45°$

C3 $a = 70°$ $b = 70°$ $c = 55°$ $d = 65°$
$e = 50°$ $f = 45°$ $g = 90°$

C4 60° because $180° ÷ 3$ is 60°

D Drawing triangles (p 119)

D1 The pupil's accurate copies of triangles with sides and angles marked

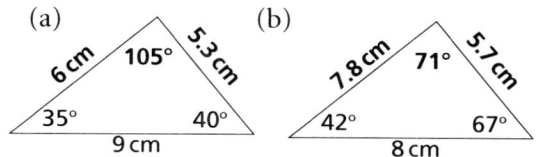

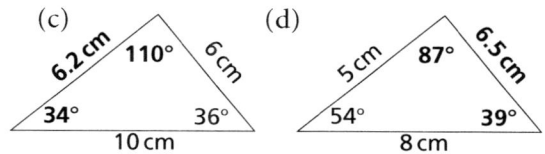

(a) (b)

(c) (d)

D2 (a) 45°
(b) The pupil's triangle
(c) 35°
The pupil's triangle

D3 The pupil's copy of the pattern

D4 (a) The pupil's scale drawing
(b) 3.1 m

D5 (a) The pupil's scale drawing
(b) $70 + 60 + 40 = 170$ m

What progress have you made? (p 122)

1 $a = 110°$ $b = 45°$ $c = 55°$

2 $a = 85°$ $b = 220°$ $c = 120°$

3 $a = 55°$ $b = 62°$ $c = 70°$

4 The pupil's accurate drawing of these triangles

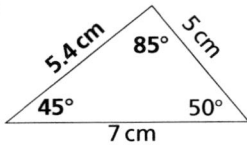

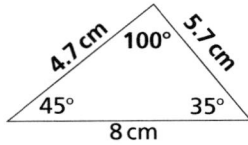

5 The pupil's net for a triangular prism
Check that sides of triangle are 5 cm long.

Practice booklet

Section A (p 50)

1 a is acute b is reflex c is acute
   d is reflex e is obtuse f is obtuse

2 A and F, B and E, C and D

3 $a = 105°$ $b = 15°$ $c = 83°$ $d = 67°$

4 (a) C, D and F   (b) A, B, D and E

Section B (p 51)

1 A and E, B and F, C and D

2 $a = 215°$ $b = 40°$ $c = 265°$
   $d = 130°$ $e = 115°$

3 40°

4 A regular dodecagon (12 sides)

5 (a) C, E and F   (b) A, B, D and E

Section C (p 52)

1 $a = 40°$ $b = 145°$ $c = 50°$ $d = 89°$

2 $a = 30°$ $b = 55°$ $c = 68°$ $d = 44°$

3 $a + b = 90°$

4 $a = 50°$ $b = 50°$ $c = 30°$
   $d = 120°$ $e = 75°$ $f = 30°$

Sections D and E (p 53)

1 The pupil's accurate drawings with these measurements:

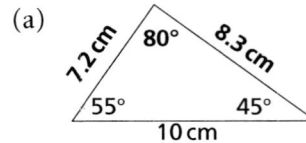

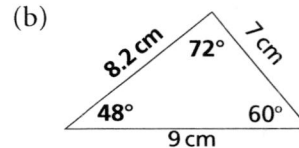

(a)

(b)

2 The pupil's accurate copy of this pattern (drawn here on a 50% scale)

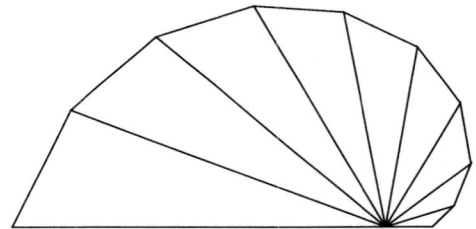

3 (a) The pupil's accurate scale drawing of tent piece

   (b) 101 cm, 120 cm

4 The pupil's accurate drawing of the net. (The base is an equilateral triangle of sides length 8 cm and the sides are isosceles triangles.)

㉑ True or false? (p 123)

◊ This unit introduces the idea of a counter-example to prove that a general statement is false. In your introduction make it clear that for a statement to be true, it must always be true; but for a statement to be false, just a single counter-example will disprove it.

The statements on the page are best discussed in groups, with each group reporting back to the whole class at the end. For any statement that is false, pupils should provide a counter-example. Though at this stage pupils are not expected to prove that a statement is true, you might ask the class to see if they could justify in words why they think a statement is true.

After discussing the examples on the page, pupils might produce their own statements for the rest of the class to discuss.

◊ More able pupils might find discussing algebraic statements interesting. For example, if n is a positive whole number, is each of the following true or false?

$4n + 1$ is odd   (Yes)
$5n + 1$ is even   (No – try $n = 2$)
$n^2 + n$ is even   (Yes)
$n^2 + n + 1$ is prime   (No – try $n = 4$)

◊ For the statements in the text:

Abby – true
Beth – false (try any decimal for example)
Callum – false (an isosceles triangle disproves this)
Dan – true
Eddie – false (try starting with 4)
Faith – true
Grace – false (try doing it!)

22 Time and timetables

Essential

Sheet 286 (or a copy of the calendar for the current year)
Sheet 287

Practice booklet pages 54 to 58 (needs sheet 286 or a copy of a calendar)

A Using a calendar (p 124)

Sheet 286 or a copy of the calendar for the current year

◊ The calendar can be used as a basis for oral work.

◊ Pupils are likely to need some support in counting the number of weeks between two dates when the dates are in different months.

◊ You may wish to use calendars in different formats to give pupils plenty of experience.

'A nice gentle start – lots of discussion about birthdays etc.'

B The 12-hour clock (p 125)

This reviews work on the 12-hour clock.

C The 24-hour clock (p 126)

Sheet 287

◊ Pupils can count twice round the large clock on page 126, starting at 1 for 1 a.m. Point out that we normally put a zero in front of times like 01:00. Once pupils are clear about how to measure 24-hour clock time, they can order the times A to I. The correct order (earliest first) is H, A, E, B, F, I, C, D, G.

◊ Although pupils may find the large clock helpful in converting to and from 24-hour time, encourage them to try questions C2 onwards without looking back at this clock.

◊ An additional activity is '24-hour clock bingo'. Pupils choose times for their 'card' from a range of 24-hour clock times. You call out the 12-hour clock times and pupils cross off corresponding 24-hour clock times.

*C9 This is likely to be a challenge for some pupils. They could work in groups and, when they think they have found the solution, they could try to communicate their reasoning as clearly as possible.

Ⅾ **Timetables** (p 128)

◊ Discuss how to interpret each timetable, emphasising that the bus timetable is read downwards but the train timetable is read across.

Pupils are likely to be more interested in local timetables, provided they are reasonably simple.

◊ Point out that 24-hour times are often written in timetables with no punctuation marks to separate hours and minutes.

Ⓐ **Using a calendar** (p 124)

(Answers for sheet 286 – the year 2000.)

A1 Wednesday

A2 (a) 6 March   (b) 26 August

A3 5

A4 18 February

A5 4 December

A6 14 April

A7 3

A8 11 July

Ⓑ **The 12-hour clock** (p 125)

B1 (a) 8:10 a.m.   (b) 1:30 p.m.
     (c) 7:45 a.m.   (d) 11:20 a.m.
     (e) 10:40 p.m.

B2 (a) 3:10 p.m.
     (b) 20 minutes
     (c) (i) 4:15 p.m.   (ii) 5 minutes
     (d) 6:00 p.m.
     (e) 1 hour 30 minutes

B3 (a) 40 minutes
     (b) 1 hour 30 minutes
     (c) 2 hours 20 minutes
     (d) 2 hours 45 minutes

B4 1 hour 15 minutes

Ⓒ **The 24-hour clock** (p 126)

C1 (a) Daisy
     (b) Bindoo and Helga,
         Carol and Francis,
         Ela and Gayarri

C2

12-hour clock	24-hour clock
2:30 p.m.	14:30
5:15 p.m.	**17:15**
6:10 a.m.	06:10
12:25 p.m.	**12:25**
9:50 p.m.	21:50
4:35 a.m.	**04:35**
6:25 p.m.	**18:25**
11:15 p.m.	23:15
10:10 a.m.	**10:10**
7:40 p.m.	**19:40**

C3 (a) 9:00 a.m.   (b) 1:10 p.m.

     (c) 11:30 a.m.   (d) 3:40 p.m.

     (e) 10:10 p.m.

C4 02:05, 6:45 a.m., 1:00 p.m., 16:00, 18:09, 8:35 p.m., 21:40

C5 (a) 30 minutes   (b) 15 minutes

     (c) 1 hour 15 minutes

     (d) 1 hour 40 minutes

C6 35 minutes

C7 1 hour 40 minutes

C8 27 minutes

*C9 (a) Pepita Pharos

     Warren's statement matches Eric's and Pablo's. Suki's statement matches Eric's and Jude's. Peg's and Pablo's statements match.

     However, Chris's and Pepita's statements do not match. Also, Doug's and Pepita's statements do not match.

     Since only one person is lying, it must be Pepita.

(b) The billiard room

     Doug was in the lounge.
     Chris was in the toilets.
     Jude (and perhaps Suki) were in the gym.
     Warren and Eric were in the bar.
     Peg was in the restaurant.
     Staff were in the kitchen.

Ⓓ **Timetables** (p 128)

D1 08:40 or 8:40 a.m.

D2 09:00 or 9:00 a.m.

D3 17 minutes

D4 09:02 or 9:02 a.m.

D5 10 minutes

D6 13:21 or 1:21 p.m.

D7 2 hours 29 minutes

D8 2 hours 29 minutes

D9 14:27

D10 12:00

D11 25 minutes

D12 4 minutes

D13 22 minutes

D14 13 minutes

D15 19:34

D16 20:34

D17 4

What progress have you made? (p 129)

1 Wednesday

2 (a) 15:20   (b) 3:30 a.m.

3 (a) 24 minutes

   (b) 20:30 or 8:30 p.m.

Practice booklet

Section A (p 54)

These answers use the year 2000 calendar.

1 Monday

2 11 August

3 4

4 23 June

5 January, April, July, September, December

6 5 August

7 30 September, 7 October, 14 October, 21 October

8 7

9 10 March, 7 April, 5 May

10 1 (13 October)

Sections B and C (p 55)

1 (a) 6:30 a.m.   (b) 11:20 a.m.
(c) 9:45 p.m.   (d) 3:50 p.m.
(e) 6:55 p.m.

2 (a) 05:15   (b) 22:20   (c) 15:30
(d) 22:45   (e) 04:40   (f) 19:50

3 (a) 03:10   (b) 16:10   (c) 14:30
(d) 10:35   (e) 12:55   (f) 22:45

4 (a) 13:20   (b) 04:20   (c) 11:50
(d) 17:25   (e) 09:00   (f) 23:30
(g) 21:05   (h) 10:30

5 (a) 6:50 a.m   (b) 1:45 p.m.
(c) 11:10 a.m.   (d) 3:10 p.m.
(e) 4:20 p.m.   (f) 6:35 p.m.
(g) 8:00 p.m.   (h) 10:15 p.m.

6 (a) 45 minutes   (b) 1 h 20 min
(c) 1 h 20 min   (d) 45 minutes
(e) 2 h 15 min   (f) 1 h 20 min

7 35 minutes

8 1 hour 20 minutes

9 18 minutes

10 2 hours 25 minutes

11 (a) 35 minutes   (b) Paul
(c) 25 minutes   (d) 15 minutes

Section D (p 57)

1 8 minutes

2 09:09

3 09:05

4 41 minutes

5 09:38

6 18 minutes

7 09:57

8 48 minutes

9 4

10 15:03

11 42 minutes

12 27 minutes

13 33 minutes

14 8 minutes

15 12:15

16 32 minutes

㉓ More negative numbers

This unit introduces adding positive and negative numbers without a
context. Subtracting a positive number is included, but not subtracting
a negative number.

p 130 **A** Hot and cold	Revision of adding and subtracting in the context of temperature
p 131 **B** From temperature to number	Moving from the context of temperature to using numbers
p 133 **C** Adding negative numbers	Additions such as $1 + {}^-2$ or ${}^-1 + {}^-2$

Practice booklet pages 59 and 60

𝔸 **Hot and cold** (p 130)

𝔹 **From temperature to number** (p 131)

◊ In the context of temperature a calculation such as ${}^-3 + 5$ can be
interpreted as a change in temperature, where the number that is added
or subtracted always represents how much the temperature rises or falls
by. In this context a calculation such as $4 + {}^-2$ does not make sense, and
will be dealt with in section C.

The changes of temperature in the introduction are:
Start at 3°C and go up by 5 degrees (to 8°C)
Start at ${}^-3$°C and go down by 5 degrees (to ${}^-8$°C)
Start at ${}^-3$°C and go up by 5 degrees (to 2°C)

ℂ **Adding negative numbers** (p 133)

◊ It is important to make the distinction between ${}^-3$ (a quantity which in
itself is negative, such as a temperature or a negative score) and $- 3$
(which means subtract the positive number 3). In the SMP Interact
books, the difference is emphasised by the negative sign always being
raised.

◊ When trialling, several teachers held joke contests, with pupils as judges
awarding points from ${}^-10$ to 10. Teachers who did this found their pupils
then understood adding and subtracting directed numbers better. If you
need to tell some jokes to set the ball rolling, here are some suggestions
(of suitably varied quality):

Q: What do you call a camel with three humps?
A: Humphrey

Q: What did the policeman say to his tummy?
A: You're under a vest.

Q: What did the Spanish farmer say to his chickens?
A: Ole!

Focus first on the fact that when you add a set of numbers together any negative number in the set pulls the total score down. Using a number line, such as that on page 131, will be useful here.

Check that pupils realise it does not matter which way round you add numbers; for example ⁻3 + 5 is equal to 5 + ⁻3.

These are the totals for the pictures on the lower half of page 133:

(a) 2   (b) ⁻8   (c) ⁻2   (d) ⁻2   (e) 1   (f) ⁻3

C8 If pupils have not met magic squares before, you may need to demonstrate with one that has, for example, the numbers 1 to 9 in it; its magic number will be 15. Point out that no number is used twice.

Ⓐ **Hot and cold** (p 130)

A1 (a) ⁻10°C   (b) 0°C

A2 ⁻5°C

A3 29 degrees

A4 128 degrees

A5 (a) 3°C   (b) ⁻2°C   (c) 400 m
     (d) 100 m   (e) 1100 m

Ⓑ **From temperature to number** (p 131)

B1 J and S (3°C), K and U (⁻3°C),
L and R (5°C), M and T (⁻5°C)

B2 (a) ⁻2 + 3 = **1**   (b) ⁻6 + 2 = **⁻4**
     (c) ⁻8 + 8 = **0**   (d) ⁻8 + 10 = **2**
     (e) ⁻1 + 2 = **1**   (f) ⁻2 + 5 = **3**
     (g) ⁻3 + 5 = **2**   (h) ⁻1 + 6 = **5**

B3 (a) 3 − 2 = **1**   (b) 3 − 4 = **⁻1**
     (c) ⁻5 − 4 = **⁻9**   (d) ⁻3 − 3 = **⁻6**
     (e) 0 − 4 = **⁻4**   (f) 4 − 7 = **⁻3**
     (g) ⁻7 − 4 = **⁻11**   (h) ⁻3 − 0 = **⁻3**

B4 (a) ⁻3 + 2 = **⁻1**   (b) ⁻2 − 8 = **⁻10**
     (c) ⁻5 + 4 = **⁻1**   (d) ⁻6 − 2 = **⁻8**
     (e) 3 − 7 = **⁻4**   (f) ⁻7 + 3 = **⁻4**
     (g) ⁻1 − 5 = **⁻6**   (h) ⁻3 + 3 = **0**

B5 (a) 2 − 6   (b) 1 − 4
     (c) ⁻2 + 3   (d) 0 − 3

B6 (a) 2 − **3** = ⁻1   (b) 2 − **4** = ⁻2
     (c) 2 − **5** = ⁻3   (d) **2** − 7 = ⁻5
     (e) ⁻4 − **1** = ⁻5   (f) **7** − 5 = 2
     (g) **8** − 10 = ⁻2   (h) **8** − 4 = 4

B7 (a) **⁻8** + 3 = ⁻5   (b) **⁻2** + 4 = 2
     (c) 4 + **3** = 7   (d) 4 − **11** = ⁻7

B8 (a) 50 − 60 = **⁻10**
     (b) ⁻30 − 50 = **⁻80**
     (c) **⁻40** − 60 = ⁻100
     (d) ⁻90 + **80** = ⁻10
     (e) 15 − **115** = ⁻100
     (f) 100 − **121** = ⁻21
     (g) **60** − 18 = 42
     (h) ⁻63 + **48** = ⁻15

'The best joke we had was: "Why was Cinderella never chosen for the football team?" … "Because she had a pumpkin for a coach!"'

B9 (a) 2, 0, $^-2$ and the pupil's explanation

(b) $^-1$, $^-3$, $^-5$ and the pupil's explanation

(c) 0, $^-10$, $^-20$ and the pupil's explanation

(d) $^-10$, $^-12$, $^-14$ and the pupil's explanation

(e) The pupil's questions

B10 $15 - 20$

B11 Three of
$^-4 + 6 = 2$, $^-4 + 5 = 1$, $^-4 + 3 = ^-1$,
$^-4 + 2 = ^-2$, $^-4 + 1 = ^-3$

B12 Three of
$3 - 6 = ^-3$, $3 - 5 = ^-2$, $3 - 2 = 1$,
$3 - 1 = 2$

ℂ Adding negative numbers (p 133)

C1 (a) $^-1$ (b) $^-11$ (c) 0   (d) $^-1$

C2 Ewan (total 1); Iain got $^-2$

C3 (a) $^-2$ (b) $^-11$ (c) 0

C4 (a) 0   (b) 6   (c) 6

C5 (a) $^-3$ (b) 3   (c) $^-4$

(d) $^-4$ (e) 4   (f) $^-3$

(g) 6   (h) 7   (i) 3

C6 3°C

C7 $^-3$°C

C8 (a)

4	$^-$**1**	0
$^-$**3**	1	**5**
2	3	$^-$**2**

(b)

1	**6**	$^-1$
0	2	**4**
5	$^-$**2**	3

(c)

$^-$2	3	$^-4$
$^-3$	$^-$**1**	**1**
2	$^-$**5**	0

What progress have you made? (p 135)

1 (a) $^-3$°C   (b) $^-17$°C

2 (a) $^-4$°C   (b) 2°C

3 (a) 3   (b) $^-2$ (c) $^-4$

(d) $^-8$ (e) 0   (f) 3

4 (a) 2   (b) $^-5$ (c) $^-3$

(d) $^-2$ (e) $^-5$ (f) $^-5$

5 (a) $^-2$ (b) $^-3$ (c) $^-2$ (d) $^-6$

Practice booklet

Section A (p 59)

1 5°C

2 (a) 2°C   (b) $^-2$°C   (c) $^-1$°C   (d) $^-20$°C

3 It rose by 27 degrees.

4 There are many possibilities, for example:
A temperature of 3°C is 9 degrees higher than a temperature of $^-6$°C.
A temperature of $^-9$°C is 6 degrees lower than a temperature of $^-3$ °C.

5 $^-5$°C, $^-4$°C, $^-1$°C, 0°C, 1°C, 2°C, 9°C

Section B (p 59)

1 $6 - 8 = ^-2$

2 (a) $^-2 + 5 = $ **3**   (b) $^-1 + 10 = $ **9**

(c) $^-3 + 9 = $ **6**   (d) $^-6 + 8 = $ **2**

3 (a) $2 - 5 = $ **$^-3$**   (b) $1 - 9 = $ **$^-8$**

(c) $^-3 - 1 = $ **$^-4$**   (d) $^-6 - 3 = $ **$^-9$**

4 (a) $^-4 + 2 = ^-2$ (b) $^-9 + $ **6** $ = ^-3$

(c) **4** $ - 9 = ^-5$ (d) $6 - $ **18** $ = ^-12$

5 (a) 0, $^-3$, $^-6$ (b) $^-0.2$, $^-0.4$, $^-0.6$

(c) 1, 3, 5   (d) $^-2\frac{1}{2}$, $^-3$, $^-3\frac{1}{2}$

6 The pupil's three calculations with the answer $^-2$

Section C (p 60)

1 (a) $^-5$ (b) 4   (c) $^-1$

(d) $^-4$ (e) 2   (f) $^-11$

2 (a) $^-4 + ^-$**3** $ = ^-7$ (b) $^-1 + ^-$**3** $ + ^-2 = ^-6$

(c) $2 + ^-$**9** $ + ^-3 = ^-10$

3 $^-2$°C

4 (a)

$^-3$	**2**	$^-5$
$^-$**4**	$^-2$	0
1	$^-$**6**	$^-$**1**

(b)

0	**5**	$^-$**2**
$^-$**1**	1	3
4	$^-$**3**	2

(c)

3	$^-2$	$^-1$
$^-$**4**	**0**	**4**
1	2	$^-$**3**

㉔ Ratio

Pupils multiply up recipes in different contexts to maintain a ratio, and use a formal notation to write ratios.

p 136 **A** Recipes		Multiplying up ratios
p 138 **B** Ratios		Writing ratios in a written form
p 139 **C** Using shorthand		Using the standard colon notation

Optional
Multilink cubes in two colours

Practice booklet pages 61 and 62

Ⓐ **Recipes** (p 136)

There are two key ideas that need to be discussed in the introductory activity:

- To keep the same colour the ratio must be kept the same by 'multiplying up'. This can be established by asking questions such as 'How would you make twice the quantity of light orange?'
- Different oranges are made by changing the ratio of red and yellow. Darker oranges are made by increasing the proportion of red, lighter colours using a higher proportion of yellow. When pupils suggest recipes for the new shades of orange, ask them to explain why.

Ⓑ **Ratios** (p 138)

This section uses the term 'ratio' for the first time. The main idea here is that a large mixture of cubes can sometimes be seen as a collection of small blocks with exactly the same combination of colours.

Optional: multilink cubes in two colours

◊ You could show pupils some blocks made from multilink cubes of different colours. Ask them to describe the ratio in the block. Emphasise that the order is important.

◊ A collection of blocks could be prepared in advance where say the ratio of red to yellow was $2:1$. Ask pupils to guess what the ratio of red to yellow is and then test their guesses by putting the blocks together. If you have enough blocks several sets of blocks could be put together in different ratios in labelled sandwich bags. In groups, pupils could try to guess the ratio and then test their guesses. Using different sets of colours in each bag will avoid confusion and bags becoming muddled.

◊ This idea could be extended by asking pupils how a mixture of say 12 red and 4 yellow cubes could be made into a number of smaller, equal blocks.

ℂ Using shorthand (p 139)

𝔸 Recipes (p 136)

A1 (a) 6   (b) 12

A2

	Blue	Yellow
2 times the recipe	6 tins	**4 tins**
3 times the recipe	**9 tins**	**6 tins**
5 times the recipe	**15 tins**	**10 tins**
10 times the recipe	**30 tins**	**20 tins**

A3 (a) 12 litres

   (b) (i) 8 litres   (ii) 10 litres

   (c) 5 litres

A4 (a) 8 litres

   (b) (i) 20 litres   (ii) 25 litres

A5

Litres of blue	Litres of yellow	Litres of light green
4	10	14
6	15	21
8	20	28
10	25	35

A6 (a) 3   (b) 450 g

   (c) 1500 g or 1.5 kg

   (d) Spinach Sauté
     (Serves 6)
     1500 g fresh spinach
     450 g unsalted peanuts
     3 large onions
     450 g margarine

A7 Spinach Sauté
   (Serves 4)
   1000 g fresh spinach
   300 g unsalted peanuts
   2 large onions
   300 g margarine

A8 (a) 250 g   (b) 75 g

A9 (a) 12   (b) 500 g

   (c) 125 g   (d) 375 g

𝔹 Ratios (p 138)

B1 (a) 3 to 1   (b) 1 to 2

   (c) 1 to 3   (d) 4 to 1

B2 (a) No   (b) Yes

   (c) 1 to 2   (d) 2 to 1

B3 (a) Set E; ratio 2 to 1

   (b) Set D; ratio 3 to 1

ℂ Using shorthand (p 139)

C1 (a) 1:3   (b) 2:1   (c) 3:2

C2 (a) 1:5   (b) 4:1

   (c) 3:2   (d) 3:4

C3 (a) 1:4   (b) 3:1   (c) 3:2

C4 The ratio of green tea to dried mint = 2:1

What progress have you made? (p 140)

1 (a) 15 litres (b) 5 litres

2 (a) 1:4 (b) 2:5

Practice booklet

Section A (p 61)

1 (a) 6 (b) 8

2 (a) (i) 4 litres (ii) 6 litres
   (b) $\frac{1}{2}$ litre

3 (a) 300 g (b) 12 tbsp (c) 50 g

4 Shortbread
   (makes 24 pieces)
   450 g plain flour
   9 tbsp rice flour
   150 g caster sugar
   300 g butter

Section B (p 62)

1 (a) 2 to 1 (b) 1 to 2 (c) 3 to 2

2 (a) Yes (b) No
   (c) The ratio of black to white is **1** to **4**.
       The ratio of white to black is **4** to **1**.

Section C (p 62)

1 (a) 1:3 (b) 2:3 (c) 3:1

2 (a) 1:6 (b) 3:2 (c) 1:5

3 The ratio of geraniums to lobelias = 1:3

Review 4 (p 141)

1 $a = 65°$ $b = 125°$ $c = 75°$

2 (a) **13** is a prime number.
   (b) **36** is a multiple of 12.
   (c) **9** is a factor of 45.
   (d) **8** is the square root of **64**.
   (e) **35** has 5 as a factor.

3 (a) TRUE
   (b) FALSE and the pupil's example
   (c) FALSE and the pupil's example

4 (a) 35 minutes
   (b) 1 hour 45 minutes
   (c) 45 minutes
   (d) 3 hours 25 minutes

5 (a) $^-3 + 7 = \mathbf{4}$ (b) $^-8 + 5 = {}^-\mathbf{3}$
   (c) $^-3 + \mathbf{5} = 2$ (d) $^-7 + \mathbf{4} = {}^-3$
   (e) $^-3 - 7 = {}^-10$ (f) $3 - 5 = {}^-2$
   (g) $2 + {}^-7 = {}^-\mathbf{5}$ (h) $8 + {}^-5 = 3$
   (i) $7 + {}^-\mathbf{3} = 4$ (j) $5 + {}^-7 = {}^-2$
   (k) $7 + {}^-2 + 5 = \mathbf{10}$
   (l) $^-6 + 10 + {}^-2 = \mathbf{2}$

6 $\frac{4}{12} = \frac{1}{3}$

7 (a) 5 right and 4 up
   (b) 7 right and 1 down
   (c) 7 left and 5 up
   (d) (None across and) 4 down

8 (a) 3 tbs   (b) 1000 g or 1 kg
   (c) 400 g   (d) 100 ml

9 (a) $\frac{8}{13}$ (b) $\frac{1}{2}$ (c) $\frac{2}{9}$ (d) $\frac{1}{3}$

10 (a) 1 : 3 (b) 3 : 2 (c) 3 : 1

11 (a) 17   (b) 41   (c) $b = 4p + 1$

Mixed questions 4 (Practice booklet p 63)

1 (a) a, d and f (b) b and e
   (c) c and g

2 The pupil's accurate drawing, showing
   these measurements:

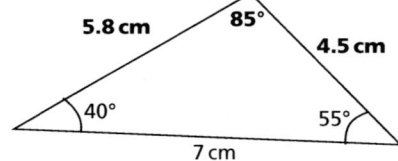

3 (a) True
   (b) False (it could be a rhombus)
   (c) True

4 (a) 1st September   (b) 10 nights

5 (a) 1   (b) 4   (c) $^-5$ (d) 0
   (e) 1   (f) $^-2$ (g) $^-1$ (h) $^-7$

6 12 degrees

7 (a) 3 minutes   (b) 3:43 p.m. or 1543
   (c) 30 minutes   (d) 1524

8 (a) 3 : 1   (b) 2 : 1   (c) 2 : 3

9 (a) 50 g   (b) 75 ml
   (c) Lemon Surprise Pudding (serves 12)
       75 g butter
       300 g caster sugar
       6 eggs
       rind and juice of 3 lemons
       450 ml milk
       75 g plain flour